THE BRIDGE GENERATION

A queer elders' chronicle from no rights to civil rights

QUIRK-E

Contents

Preface

Wayson Choy

I have almost died twice. How can I urge you to take a chance to explore your life fully? First, read these writers - they show you how to start, how it's done. Second, try writing your own truth. Through the seven years of the Quirk-e writing workshops, the group has raised the literary standards they demand from each other. The evolving well-crafted short stories are written by long-term members and by those who have - in fact - been published before in many other journals. Yet, these experienced writers are proudly published alongside those who are just learning to find their narrative voice. This has been true with their collective public readings, their successful exhibit of digital images, their 'human library,' their memory boxes, and their risk-taking creative stage performances. Every brave voice deserves a hearing. If you have ever felt you have been targeted as 'the other,' ever felt abandoned, mocked for being different, here are individual voices that may connect with you. From what seems very simply stated work, deceptively light in theme, you will confront writers that have evolved and matured into taking even deeper risks to tell of the secrets and truths often denied or buried by our families and society. And in these pages you will discover, too, the pleasure of a witty phrase or the deeper reward of a freshly honed point of view. This edition may intensely inspire you because what is collectively revealed remains utterly human and vulnerable. In short, you are different, yes, and you are not alone.

Introduction

Claire Robson

Since history is the narrative of victors, each word in this anthology represents a small triumph. At the time their authors were born, such words could not have been written or barely imagined. We remember being damned by our churches, rejected by our friends and parents, fired from our jobs, and beaten on the streets. Whether or not these things happened to us as individuals, we lived in the shadow of their possibility, and though many of us are out and proud today, we still recall those times of fear and shame. We were born *pre Ellen, pre Stonewall, pre Internet, pre Pride.* Many saw us as sick criminals who should be kept away from children - even our own. We crept through libraries and bookstores hunting for any mention of our name, our identity, and our condition. Some of us hid. Some of us stood out. Whatever we did and however we lived, we were part of a long queer journey - from no rights to civil rights.

We have written this book in order to make our stories and histories part of the record. They are complicated stories because these were complicated times – times of fear, for sure, but also times of glory and excitement, in which we invented bent and beautiful strategies of resistance, survival, and celebration. If there's one thing we have learned, it's that conformity does not save us. Rather, we must stay dedicated to queerness. Being creatively *quirk-e* isn't just a charming hobby for oldies; it's a passionate resistance to staying straight, keeping quiet, and hoping for the best. It was what we did to stay alive and kicking in inhospitable and dangerous times.

Quirk-e began in 2006 with a happy coincidence. I was new to town and looking to network. Chris Morrissey was in charge of programming at the Generations Project. We put together a series of workshops at the old 411 Senior Centre on Dunsmuir Street in Vancouver.

How quickly things got out of hand!

By the end of six weeks the group had begun to morph into a band of *artivists* - artist activists writing back to stereotypes about being old and queer. Instead of being an in-charge writing teacher, I had become more like a pirate captain – negotiating precarious consensus among a band of opinionated peers. When it came to the final session, my 'students' refused to go away. In a stroke of queer ingenuity, Chris brokered our acceptance into the Arts, Health & Seniors' Project – a pilot managed by Vancouver Park Board. Thanks to their commitment to free long-term arts experiences for seniors, we had three years of support and funding – a treat for a generation used to meeting in church basements and friends' living rooms. In those three luxurious years, we coined our name, revised our mission, and invented brand new ways of working together.

Today, Quirk-e finds its own funding - at the time of writing we are operating on a generous Cultural Grant from the City of Vancouver. We're also supported by our valued community partners – Britannia Community Services Centre, which donates meeting space and staff support, and QMUNITY Generations, which handles registrations and provides a budget for weekly snacks. Thirty of us work with both images and text to make art that notices everything - the sags and wrinkles, the moments of grace, the beautiful and the absurd. We remain constantly precarious - a discordant choir that welcomes differences, conflicts, and irreconcilable points of view.

We hope you will enjoy the stories in this collection. They are the product of two years' collective work. We began by researching each of the decades – scouring the Vancouver Public Library for the music, news, and queer experiences of the times. We then brainstormed writing prompts and wrote for a full year before peer reviewing the results and making a final selection. Every member of the group at the time of writing the anthology is represented here.

We are indebted to many people. Dr. Elise Chenier has been an important teacher and ally throughout the writing process. She also contributed the excellent contextual overview that precedes each section. Canadian author Wayson Choy has been our friend and mentor since our inception; he donated seed money to the project and was the first to suggest that our stories needed to be properly published and disseminated across Canada. We offer love and homage to jill weaving from the Vancouver Parks Board and Claire Gram from Vancouver Coastal Health who began the Arts & Health Project, and to Margaret Naylor, also from Vancouver Parks Board. Margaret and jill continue to work tirelessly to support this and many other arts experiences for Vancouver's seniors. Thanks also to Anne Jackson, our most gracious host at Britannia's Seniors' Lounge. In 2011, we were joined by artist intern Kelsey Blair, who is now co-lead artist for the group, and co-editor of this collection.

Finally, our thanks to Willeen Keogh and the department of Gender, Sexuality, and Women's Studies at Simon Fraser University for their sponsorship of the anthology. This completes a circle for many of us. Years ago, in the words of Lord Alfred Douglas, our love "dared not speak its name." Today, we are happy, grateful, and proud to published under the SFU logo – an important and significant step for the members of the Bridge Generation.

About the 1940s and 1950s

Elise Chenier

The 1940s and 50s may well be the two most important decades in the modern history of sexuality. These were the years when the notion that homosexuality was a mental disease and a public safety threat fully penetrated popular culture in the English-speaking western world, and yet at the same time, finding and participating in same-sex social networks became much easier for women, men, and trans* people, particularly for those of white heritage.

Few lives were untouched by the war. For men, war meant an opportunity to escape the economic hardship of the Great Depression either through paid employment in the proliferating munitions factories, or by joining the service. The demand for labour was so great that women too were major beneficiaries of the European conflict. Overnight they were provided with seemingly endless opportunities to learn trades and occupy positions normally reserved for men. They earned wages close to or on par with men, something that was never seen before, nor has been seen since. Women's increased participation in the workplace on the home front, and women and men's involvement in the military, allowed for the proliferation of same-sex and queer social networks. Consequently, lesbian, gay and trans* culture and communities expanded in new ways, and into new regions. Ports like San Francisco and heavily industrialized cities like Detroit and Toronto were just some of the sites of increasingly visible public queer cultures.

People of white and non-white heritage experienced these changes differently. In the late 1930s and early 1940s, many non-whites saw the war as an opportunity to win full citizenship rights for once and for all.

Indigenous people, Chinese and African Canadian and American men believed that by fighting in the war against totalitarianism alongside whites they could no longer be denied social and civil rights at home. Changes to laws that overtly discriminated against people of Chinese heritage were eliminated as a result of pressure exerted by the newly created United Nations, but racial prejudice remained more or less intact at war's end. People of colour were as likely to experience racism in gay clubs and in the barracks as they were in department stores and the cinema. Consequently, people of colour and whites developed separate social networks.

Psychiatrists also saw opportunity in the war. They convinced the U.S. government that they could help build a better, stronger, fighting force by eliminating those recruits who showed personality disorders. Testing for signs of abnormal sexuality became part of the induction process, and in 1941 the United States Army Surgeon General's office officially classified 'homosexual proclivities' as disqualifying inductees from military service. Women and men found, or suspected of having engaged, in same-sex sex were discharged. In the United States, and perhaps Canada as well, people of African heritage were disproportionately affected by this policy. For all ethnic groups, anything other than an honorable discharge had terrible consequences. The stigma attached to being homosexual only worsened after the war, and those discharged for homosexuality were excluded from the benefits packages others received.

The idea that homosexuality was a mental disease became part of mainstream culture as a direct result of psychiatrists' involvement in the military's induction process. Psychiatrists also propagated the notion that gay men could not control their sexual desires, and that they often sought out young boys as sexual companions, thus giving rise to the idea the gay men are pedophiles. People once considered merely *queer* now appeared to be a serious danger to the public, especially children. Lesbians were less likely to be arrested and subject to mental health and criminal laws that were aimed at *curing* homosexuals, but they too lived under the shadow of fear and stigma. They were also regarded as mentally ill. Indeed, many women who grew up in this era loathe the word *lesbian*, so strongly do they associate it with illness.

For trans* people, the increased influence of the sexual sciences had positive effects. On December 1, 1952 the *New York Daily News'* headline announced "Ex-GI Becomes Blonde Beauty." Christine Jorgenson's transition from male to female was heralded as a marvel of scientific progress and human innovation. Trans* surgical techniques were still experimental and often painful at this time, but access to such treatment was a tremendous advance for many trans* people. Of course, the high cost of surgery put it out of reach for most, but Jorgenson helped legitimate transsexuality as a legitimate experience and identity, and she became a positive role model for many trans and queer people for the next two decades. Rather than representing a cultural acceptance of sex and gender fluidity, however, media coverage of Jorgenson's sex change contributed to the hardening of the differences between the sexes. Science, the media pronounced, could fix what nature got wrong. In this way, Jorgenson's gender and sexuality was made to conform to existing heterosexual norms. Homosexuals and other queers remained sex and gender freaks and misfits.

Heterosexuals celebrated war's end by embracing marriage and family life, and the baby boom followed to prove it. Psychological ideas about sex and gender norms developed over the previous decade were adopted by teachers and parents eager to raise a generation built for peace, not conflict. Modern approaches to child development enjoyed a ready audience; in the 1950s, children whose choice of clothes and games did not conform to their biological sex found themselves subject to the critical gaze of professionals eager to help them make the social adjustment to their lives as future husbands and wives. Many gays and lesbians first encountered these attitudes well before their first same-sex kiss; they encountered them when playing dress-up involved choosing clothes of the opposite sex, or when their declared future ambitions were not congruent with their assigned gender role.

If one did not encounter negative judgment in school or at home, the church was there to fill the breech. Organized religion affirmed the notion that anything other than gender conformity and heterosexuality was a sin against God. Sermons from the pulpit, Sunday school teachings, and Bible camps all provided constant reminders that queers were an abomination. The levee broke in the mid-50s when a United Kingdom governmental committee, in which leading members of the Church of

England participated, publicly called for a softening of attitude toward homosexuals. Over the next two decades, mainline churches would begin to re-think their position with respect to lesbians and gays and would slowly welcome them back into the community of believers.

The Cold War, however, kept such changes at bay until at least the end of the decade. The notion that homosexuals were susceptible to blackmail by Soviet agents became official government policy in Canada and the United States. Campaigns to root out gays and lesbians from the civil service are often referred to as 'witch-hunts,' and for good reason. The House Un-American Activities Committee destroyed the lives of thousands of people by publicly accusing them of communist sympathies. Because homosexuals were believed to suffer from 'character weakness,' they were thought to be susceptible to such ideological influences. Moreover, their sexual habits made them perfect targets for blackmail. Of course, there are no known cases of homosexual civil servants being blackmailed by Soviet agents, but the myth persisted. Hostility toward lesbians, gays, and trans* people was so intense and overt during the Cold War era that many queers lived in total isolation, often unaware that there were other queer people and too fearful to try and find out. Of those who discovered others like themselves, most survived by living a *double life*: they passed as heterosexual, only revealing their homosexual life when among friends *in the know*.

The unprecedented level of fear and hostility toward gender and sexual nonconformism makes it all the more remarkable that a vibrant, public queer culture took root in many major urban centres. Bars, coffeehouses and other commercial venues became hangouts for lesbians, gays, bisexuals and trans* people. Often it was only *skid row* establishments that tolerated queer people, but high-class clubs, bars and hotels such as Toronto's Letros and the Hotel Vancouver also became known as queer hotspots. Whether *high* or *low* class, public social spaces allowed people to form community networks that were, in turn, able to collectively resist police harassment and social opprobrium.

Other modes of communicating and organizing also emerged. In 1947, Edith Eyde, a typist for a Hollywood production studio, used her free time on the job to start the first known American lesbian newsletter, *Vice Versa*. Published under the clever pseudonym 'Lisa Ben,' Eyde started it shortly after she was questioned during a police raid at a gay club; she hoped *Vice Versa* would provide a safer way to meet other gay women. In Toronto, Jim Egan single-handedly launched a letter and article-writing campaign to challenge the media's homophobia and re-educate the public about what it means to be gay. In San Francisco, *ONE* and the *Daughters of Bilitis*, organizations devoted to challenging discrimination and misinformation about lesbians and gay life, were launched. All these individuals and groups pushed back against those who characterized homosexuals as pathologically sick and deviant. Many of these people were deeply inspired by the black civil rights movement and its leader, Martin Luther King, who challenged the oppression of African Americans. Just as King's movement found supporters in the white community, so too did early homophile movement members court supporters among heterosexuals, including experts like Evelyn Hooker who were willing to publicly challenge the *American Psychiatric Association*'s classification of homosexuality as a mental disease.

The 1940s and 1950s were both difficult and exciting times for queer people. How one's life unfolded depended on a kaleidoscope of variables. Shame, stigma and isolation meant that lots of people simply never 'came out.' For others, however, the discovery of a book, a night club, or coffeehouse where queers hung out, or even just a friend who had other friends like oneself, was the key that unlocked the door to the gay world, as it was called. Some would give up respectability to live in that world full time, but most would adjust themselves to the double life, living straight by day and queer by night.

Homophobic Homo

Bill Morrow and Judy Fletcher

Max Dexall

Marsha Ablowitz

When I was nine, a man with dark wavy hair and an accent came for dinner. He brought expensive chocolates and planted a soft wet kiss on my cheek.

Mom said, "This is Uncle Max Dexall."

I wiped my cheek with my sleeve.

"Call me Cousin Max," he told me years later when I visited for tea. "Uncle sounds too old." He flashed a smile and pulled up his pant leg to show off his thin ankle and smooth calf. "You should see me in my emerald heels and matching evening gown. No one has legs as beautiful as mine." Later, friends told me about his fabulous dress collection, and I regretted being too shy to ask him to take me upstairs to unlock his mahogany wardrobe.

Max was born in 1907 in Antepol, the Gorodno district of Belarus on the Polish Russian border. His grandfather was a poor Jewish farmer who painted and decorated churches to make a little extra money. After Max's death, my elderly cousin Melvin showed me a family photo of Max with his mother and four siblings standing barefoot outside a log house on a rutted dirt street. Melvin said the house had a dirt floor.

Around 1915, the Russian Czar sent Cossacks to brutalize the Jewish *Schtetl* in Belarus and evict them from their property. Max was a young teenager when they murdered his father. He escaped to Canada, and later, thanks to money sent by my great-grandmother Sara Goldberg, his family joined him. They were very poor but managed to start a boarding house in Vancouver. Max earned money through odd jobs – selling newspapers on the street and helping in relatives' shoe stores. He worked hard and managed to save a thousand dollars, which he used to open his own shoe store in the 400-block of Main Street. This was in 1928. Within a few years, a large bank wanted his desirable corner location, so the bank officials agreed to move his store, which ended up at 10th and Granville.

Max Dexall's Shoe Store was known throughout the city. Max displayed the latest styles. He was effusive with his European accent and manners; he knew all his customers by name, and when a new mother came to buy her baby's first pair of shoes, Max would kiss the little one on the forehead and give her the baby shoes for free. "I love to pay for the baby's first shoes. And this way the customers are happy and they always come back," said Max.

Cousin Melvin told me, "In the early days here in Vancouver Max organized surprise parties for the whole family almost every month. But we didn't all like him. He was sort of effeminate, and when he didn't get married, the parties stopped. Our family didn't get along so well. Max must have felt badly that he was not invited to family weddings, bar mitzvahs or Seders."

My Dad came home once from helping decorate the windows at Max's shoe store. I heard him laughing nervously and complaining to my mom.

"Well. Did anyone do anything to you?" asked my mom.

"No," said my dad. "But I was nervous down there with Max and all those fairies."

I got very excited but also confused. "Dad, Dad, did you really see a fairy? Is Uncle Max really a fairy?"

"Not that kind of fairy, a different kind. You know, a homo."

"Don't use that word, Myron," said my mother.

"Well, what should I call them, then?" asked my dad.

"I don't know," said Mom.

Years later Max took me and my partner to a fancy ocean view restaurant. He delicately cut his lettuce with the silver cutlery, winked at the waiter, and in a sexy whisper explained how he stayed involved with the Jewish Community after his family rejected him.

"Marsha, I went to the *Shara Tzedeck* every *Shabbas* to pray, and I cruised in the men's section of the synagogue. There were lots of gay Jewish men there, so sexy in their silk *tallisos*. Most of them married to hide. This was the 1950's, before Gay Liberation."

Cute lively young men came to work at Max's shoe store. He was their boss, their mentor, maybe their lover. Vancouver's drag queens came to try on high heels. Max ordered extra-large sizes in the latest styles.

"I told those queens how lovely and how feminine they looked. Marsha you can only imagine them, six-foot beefy hunks wobbling round the store trying to walk in their high heels. None of those queens had legs as beautiful as mine. You should have seen me in my emerald gown."

Max loved to tell the romantic story of how he first met George Hill.

"One day during WWII, I was working in the store. Suddenly a tall, handsome, air force man walked in. I shooed the other sales boys away and rushed to serve him myself – I always fell for men in uniform."

As soon as George left the air force, Max offered him a job at the store and personally trained him. They fell in love. For forty years, they ran the shoe store and attended concerts and the opera. They happily redecorated their home on 38th near Granville. As a young woman, I'd wander through their manicured garden with bright red and golden tulips and ornate metal garden furniture. In the art-cluttered house, I stepped gingerly on the Persian carpets. I stared at the oil paintings, the statues, and the rooms filled with gleaming antique wooden furniture. Max and George even hired a young gay artist to hand paint the kitchen wallpaper with columns of colored birds and flowering vines. Off the entry hall was a red walled Chinese den with large porcelain lion dogs and gilt flowered vases. The living room was crowded with rose crystal and dozens of Royal Doulton figurines. There was a needlepoint ladies' screen near the fireplace.

"This is to protect the ladies' pancake makeup from melting in the heat of the fire," whispered Max.

"My mother told me to never clean a dirty house," Max said. "She told me to always clean a clean house, so I put on my frilly housewife's apron and get out my red feather duster."

While Max enjoyed being the housewife in his fancy aprons, George complained about all of Max's *chatchkas*.

"They just collect dust," he said. George was the man of the house. He did the home repairs, took the car in for servicing and did all of the heavy gardening. "Well Max might pick the odd flower," said George. One of their neighbors was a homophobic doctor who never spoke to them but threw garbage and rotten fish over the fence into their spotless yard.

"What do you do George?" I asked.

"Nothing, there's no point!"

"But you must do something."

"Well. Very rarely, I throw it back."

In 1978, they sold the business and traveled the world, bought antiques, and enjoyed entertaining in their home and garden. George attended his Anglican Church and Max his Orthodox synagogue. In the 1980s, they helped organize the first GLBT Jewish group in Vancouver. They had some lively parties and talked about celebrating a gay Passover together, even starting a gay synagogue like the one in San Francisco. Then the young man who spearheaded the gay Jewish group was jailed for embezzling at his job. Max and George visited him in prison.

"I always dreamed of praying in a gay *minyan*, but thank G-d we never invested any money with him for that group," Max told me afterwards.

I took my little nephew, Adam, to visit Max and George in the 1980s, and they fussed over the youngster, kissing him, giving him money, feeding him ice cream and telling him stories. Adam was wide-eyed as George did magic tricks.

When I took one of my lesbian partners to meet Max, he planted a soft wet kiss on my cheek, then on hers and said, "We are so delighted to have another gay in the family. Isn't Marsha beautiful?"

"I think so," she said.

Over the years, I would bring various partners to meet Max and George. Graciously they invited us out to lunches and to dinners. One evening, they took us to the Gay Men's Chorus production of HMS Pinafore. At intermission, a dyke in a suit ran up and hugged Max.

"Max! Max! Remember when you gave my baby his first pair of shoes?"

"This always happens, wherever we go. Even in Squamish," George told us.

I started bringing all my gay Jewish friends to visit Max, and he soon became everyone's gay uncle, helping a new generation of young gay men with work, recommendations, and encouragement.

Max tracked down his own nephew, Cousin Malcolm - a professor in New York. Malcolm had finally come out, and like Max so many years earlier, Malcolm had been rejected by his family. He immediately replied to his Uncle Max, thanking him for the emotional support, and Max and George flew east to visit him.

"Malcolm is just beautiful," said Max.

"He is so smart, and he writes books," said George.

Malcolm published an essay he wrote about meeting his gay uncle, and Max showed it to everyone. Then Malcolm became sick with AIDS.

Max phoned me and invited me to come for a visit. When I arrived, Max and George told me the sad news.

"We hadn't heard from Malcolm for a long time. We kept phoning him and wondered why he didn't answer," said George.

"Finally he called back. We talked to him on the phone. Malcolm was crying, and we were crying," said Max. "He told us he was dying."

"We have been praying for him," said George.

"We wanted to fly out and see him one last time, but he said no," said Max.

When Malcolm died, Max recited *Kaddish*, the prayer for the dead. The *Kaddish* prayer glorifies God and is recited at home and in the synagogue daily. Traditionally, this prayer is recited by children for their deceased parents, and by parents who have lost a child.

"I have been saying *Kaddish* for Malcolm for a long time," Max told me.

Max died of heart failure in 1991. I told my little nephew that we wouldn't be visiting Uncle Max and George anymore.

"Well, at least George is still alive," he replied. At the Orthodox cemetery we threw dirt down onto Max's coffin and said the *Kaddish* for him the way he had said it for Malcolm.

After the funeral, we went to his and George's beautifully decorated home for the reception. It was a sunny day, and through the lacy curtains there were views of the red tulips in the garden. Everyone was talking and eating. After all the straight relatives and friends left, George and a group of old gay men leaned back on the embroidered couches in the antique-filled living room telling stories about Max. We were sipping tea from fine china cups and whiskey from crystal shot glasses. I was sitting on a tiny chair next to the ladies screen. George served fancy sandwiches and little pastries. One of the men sitting near me said he had been a high school teacher at Lord Byng. I told him I was a student there. He was a tall thin man, slightly stooped, with an English accent.

"Oh we had some great parties," he said. The other old men laughed.

"Remember when the police stopped our car and we were all in drag?"

"Remember the boys at the shoe store?"

"Remember the first Pride Parades?"

"Remember his emerald gown?"

Playing Wedding

Douglas Bacon

"Let's play wedding," said Mary-Ellen.

Mary-Ellen was my big sister. With tightly curled blond hair and a tummy that made her look what Mommy called pleasingly plump, Mary-Ellen was everything I thought a pretty girl should look like.

"Oh, goody, goody!" I jumped with excitement as we ran up the oak staircase to her bedroom.

It was the day after I'd turned four and exactly a month before Princess Elizabeth, the most beautiful princess of all, would marry Prince Philip of Greece, the handsomest man in the world. Everybody was excited, even sour-faced Mrs. Scollard next door who kept boarders. There were songs about it on the radio, and there were colour pictures of all the Royal Family in the *The Star Weekly*. Mary Ellen and I cut them out and put them in our scrapbooks.

The routine was always the same: Mary-Ellen was the bride, Princess Elizabeth, and I was the bridesmaid, Princess Margaret Rose, her younger sister. Nobody was Prince Philip 'cuz he was a man, and he didn't wear a dress.

"Can I be Princess 'Lizabeth this time?" I said as we climbed the stairs. "Pull-eeeze, Mary-Ellen? You're *always* Princess 'Lizabeth and it's not fair! It's *my* turn." I knew it was hopeless, but I still tried.

"No!" she said. Then, without even looking at me she said, "*I'm* Princess Elizabeth and *I'm* the bride 'cuz *I'm* the oldest and *I'm* the prettiest. *You're* Princess Margaret Rose 'cuz *you're* the youngest and skinny. You know that, Chrissy, so just shut up."

We weren't supposed to say shut up, but Mary-Ellen said it.

"Princess Elizabeth will be queen someday 'cuz she's the *oldest*," she said. "But Princess Margaret-Rose will never be queen. She'll *always* stay a princess. But she'll still be a princess," she said. "So if you're a princess you should be thankful. Really, Chrissy. You're such a brat sometimes!"

Mary-Ellen brought the box of dress up clothes we called Granny's Chest out of the cedar closet and put it at the foot of her bed. Then she sorted them into two piles. The bigger pile of clothes was for her, the smaller one for me. I loved looking at them:

- Granny Ferguson's Alice-blue gown that she'd worn as bridesmaid
- Great-grandma Billingsly's silver grey taffeta skirt with a bustle at the back
- Great-granny Pettigrew's hundred year-old ruffled pink waistcoat with sequins down the front
- Aunt Hattie's long white lace gloves with tiny red rhinestones up the arm
- Granny's small black kid gloves with two buttons under the wrist that she'd had when she was a little girl
- An antique Japanese silk shawl with persimmon-red fringe on three sides
- Aunt Tessie's ivory-white bonnet that tied up in a side-bow…and …

"Here, you can wear these," said Mary-Ellen. She handed me four or five things she didn't want. Then she showed me one thing she did want that didn't fit her. "…And you can wear these," she said as she handed me the purple, velvet Queen Anne slippers that had belonged to Great-granny Pettigrew when she was a little girl. Only someone with feet as small as Cinderella's could fit into them.

"I'm Cinderella. I'm Cinderella," I taunted. I knew how much Mary-Ellen liked them, but her feet were too big, like the Ugly Step-Sisters. She might be oldest, and might be queen some day, but I got to wear Queen Anne's royal purple velvet slippers!

We'd barely started playing wedding when we heard it: the sound of Mommy's black oxfords coming up the hardwood stairs. Panic united us.

"Quick, Chrissy, get out of the dress… fast," said Mary-Ellen. Her fingers and mine worked frantically to undo buttons on the Alice-blue gown that my fingers had just struggled to do up. "Hurry up, Chrissy! Hurry up!" As she pulled the dress over my head, I pulled off the gloves and slipped off the Japanese shawl.

My heart was thumping as loud as Mommy's rolling pin on the breadboard when she made pies. Mommy hated it when *I* played dress-up. She'd found us once before and we'd both got a licking. Mary-Ellen got it a lot worse than me because, according to Mommy, she'd "encouraged me" and was "old enough to know better". She'd said that if she ever caught us doing it again she'd "knock the living daylights out of us," and we knew she meant it.

I'd just got the last slipper off and was sitting on the floor with my legs crossed when Mommy marched into Mary-Ellen's room.

"There you are, Mary-Ellen!" said Mommy. "Didn't you hear me calling you? Go get the clothes off the line before it rains. Now!" Her narrowed eyes were riveted on Mary-Ellen.

"Yes Mommy. Sorry Mommy," said Mary-Ellen as she took off the hat with the side-bow and placed it on the bed. When she walked out of the room, she scrunched up her shoulders in apparent fear and remorse, but as she passed me she rolled her eyes and winked… in victory. We'd done it. Mommy hadn't found out. We wouldn't get a licking.

As soon as Mary-Ellen left the room, Mommy changed. She walked over next to me and smiled. Then she reached out her hand and let her fingers play and toy with my curly blond hair, looked me straight in the eye and lowered her head.

"Now, Chrissy," she said, "Tell Mommy. What's her little boy been up to with his sister today?"

The Girl in the Pond

Gayle Roberts

"Remember, Michael, don't let go of my hand," my mother cautioned me as the crowd surged forward towards the edge of the platform. The train belched black smoke and white steam as it entered the station, and I felt her hand tightening as she pulled me towards the opening coach doors. Soldiers, sailors, and airmen flooded out of the coaches, dropped their kitbags and swept their wives and children into their arms.

As my mother pulled me around one of the celebrating families who blocked our path, my attention changed from the coaches to the man. He was wearing an army uniform and could easily have been my father. He was big even though he was kneeling down with his arms wrapped around his daughter. He kissed her tenderly on the cheek, supported her in the crook of his arm and then stood up. With his other arm, he pulled his wife towards him and the three of them embraced. The soldier's daughter was about my age and, like me, had probably just started school as she was wearing a gray pleated skirt with matching knee-high socks and a green jacket with a crest on the breast pocket. Her shoes were black and, unlike my lace-up shoes, had narrow straps that went over her arches and buckled to the sides. But, it was her hair which I noticed in particular. It was the same colour as my own, but, unlike my short back and sides, hers was long, loosely curled, and cascaded over her shoulders to swirl around her face as she moved. And then she was gone as my mother relentlessly pulled me towards the waiting coaches.

As we got closer, I noticed other families. A few of the women held their arms outstretched while holding their loved one's hands. I could see one woman staring into the eyes of her serviceman husband. She stood transfixed by the immensity of the parting and then, in one smooth motion, he swept his kitbag onto his shoulder, followed us into the waiting coach, closed the door, lowered the window and waved. He waved until his wife could no longer be seen.

"Would you and your boy like this seat?" one of the soldiers asked my mother as he picked up his kitbag and swung it into the overhead rack.

My mother nodded. "I was worried about getting a seat. It takes awhile to get to Oxford."

"Are you visiting friends?" the soldier asked politely.

"I'm going to see my husband for the first time since he was shot. He's a paratrooper … perhaps I should say he *was* a paratrooper. He was shot in the leg on a drop in Italy." My mother then turned to me and asked, "Would you like your colouring book?"

I shook my head, pulled up my knee-high socks, and stuffed my green cap with its gold braid into the back pocket of my new-for-the-trip gray short trousers. I turned away from the soldier and stared out at the passing bombed-out buildings. I used my jacket sleeve in an attempt to clean cigarette smoke from the inside of the window but gave up when I realized that most of the grime was on the outside. Then, my attention changed to the train. Ever since I had seen it enter the station, it seemed like a huge beast held captive by unknown people who forced it against its will to do their bidding. It puffed and wheezed in protest as its masters coaxed it into motion; its wheels had complained loudly as they alternatively slipped and grabbed the rails. But, as it gained speed, I sensed its anger at being forced to drag the coaches and the people within them subsiding. It became free. Now there was only effortless motion and the soothing clack of wheels on rails.

Then my mother and I were walking through the park-like grounds of the hospital. As we walked through a grove of tall and stately trees, we discovered a pond. The path split and my mother and I separated as I chose the one that led to the water's edge. I felt at peace. It was the only place I had ever seen that didn't show the ravages of war. For a few minutes, war-torn England did not exist. As my mother walked on, I stopped and stared into the pond and looked at my reflection. I stared at long, loosely curled hair that cascaded over my shoulders and swirled around my face when I moved. And then, through misted eyes, I saw my shoes were black and had narrow straps, which went over my arches and buckled to the sides.

"Come on Michael," my mother said, as she waited where the two paths rejoined. "Stop daydreaming. Don't you want to see your father?"

The girl in the pond stared back at me for a moment longer, and then we parted. My mother and I walked across a lawn to the hospital. Once, it had been a stately home but, at the beginning of the war, it had been commandeered as a rehabilitation hospital for wounded servicemen. My father's bed was in a large room that opened onto a garden. His leg was wrapped in white bandages, held up at an angle by pulleys attached to the ceiling, and his upper body was encased in plaster which, when I tapped on it, sounded like a drum. Strangely, I felt reassured; the solidity of the plaster confirmed that he was alive.

"Do you want to play cowboys and Indians?" my father asked, pulling me across the bed where I was sitting and onto his cast where I now found myself astride a horse. He bounced me up and down as best he could and I broke into bouts of laughter as I slapped the sides of my horse with my hands and dug my spurs into the bed. We played horsy until my father could play no longer.

"Do you want to play in the garden?" my father asked.

"Can I play by the pond?"

"You won't be safe there," my mother said. "You can play anywhere you like in the garden as long as you're not out of sight."

As I climbed one of the many trees in the garden, I could see my mother and father talking while she held his hand in both of hers. Then, it was time to go home. My mother hugged my father as best she could and kissed him. I climbed once more onto his cast and tapped it several times. Despite my protests, my father rubbed his stubbled chin across my face and deposited a wet kiss on my cheek. Then we left.

We didn't walk through the grove of trees, but the girl in the pond was with me. I couldn't see her clearly in the train's smoke-stained window. But she was with me.

The Wizard

Chris Spencer

When I was 12, I was really angry. I'd passed the eleven plus exam, which meant I'd go to the grammar school, but yet again all the promises were broken. No dog, no bicycle, no school trip to France. I responded with non co-operation and got ready for a long struggle.

One day, my cousin Geoff gave me an old copy of one of his comics. *The Wizard* was its name. I wanted more feats of male prowess, but I didn't have the pocket money. I didn't receive any because I refused Mum's terms of exchange. The cost of this weekly comic was threepence, the exact fare of a single bus journey to school, three miles away. I began walking to school once a week, saving the fare, and buying a copy of *The Wizard*. I did it for months. I was totally identified with these male heroic types and particularly drawn to Wilson, who could leap over tall buildings and run marathons with a broken ankle.

I think you get the idea.

My *Wizard* reading was interrupted when Mum discovered a pile of them behind my wardrobe. Upon interrogation, I confessed that I had walked home from school one day a week. She told the newsagent that I wasn't allowed to read such rubbish and that he was not to sell me any more comics. She thought that that was the end of the affair.

The newsagent took pity on me and I promised never to tell - that I continued to buy and read *The Wizard*, smuggling it into the house rolled up in my sleeve and giving it away afterwards so Mum would never know.

Class Ring

Chris Morrissey

Another day at school.

I was always the last one to be picked for a team. As if my immigrant accent wasn't enough, I was always a little fatter than the other girls, and I couldn't hit a baseball to save my life. There'd been no Halloween trick or treating back in England, and no big birthday parties or Friday night trips to the movies with classmates. I learned to adapt, climbing out the window to go to the movies and seldom arriving home at the time I was told. I learned by listening in.

Today, it had been all about boys.

Amy had begun the conversation at recess. "Who do you have a crush on?" It wasn't directed at anyone in particular.

Leslie was first, "I think Archie's cute, and besides he's Father Green's golden haired boy. Maybe, if Father Green knows, I'll get better marks!" They all laughed, and I held my breath. No way was I going to say how I really felt!

Just the weekend before, Leslie had asked me to go for a drive with her. She was the only girl in the class with a driver's license. She got to drive her father's Chevy Impala with power steering. I loved watching her hands as she turned the steering wheel. So effortless. So intriguing. We'd gone back to class and said nothing.

When school was over, there was no choice but to drag my way home. I was trudging down the alley when I heard the sirens. As I got a little closer, I saw the smoke rising. It was coming from the roof of our house.

After the firefighters left, we all went in.

I saw black everywhere. Walls, counters - every surface was covered in soot. My dad pointed helplessly at his most precious possession, a hand carved crucifix that had travelled with us from England. The smell! I could hardly breathe.

I got out as fast as I could. Heart beating. Would I ever go home again?

Dad sprang into action. He ran to a neighbour's house and called his boss.

I had met Bob Shields a few times – a short man, even when he stood up straight. His clothes always looked new to me: pastel coloured Brooks Brothers Shirts with button down collars, beige trousers, always well-pressed. My dad bought his clothes from the Simpson Sears catalogue. His trousers were baggy and shiny, and he only wore a jacket and tie when we went to mass on Sundays. He worked hard, but I guess he didn't earn a whole lot. Mr. Shields drove a shiny black Buick Electra 225 Riviera 4-door Sedan. We had a second-hand '52 Chevy.

Before the firemen left, Dad gathered us all together. He told us that we would be staying in a motel for a couple of days, and after that we'd move to Mr. Shields' house. Mr. Shields would move in with Bobbie, his new girlfriend.

The fruits of sin.

Although my dad had tried to keep his boss's divorce hush-hush, I'd overhead him talking to Mom, "Imagine! At his age! I mean I know they're not Catholic - but living with another woman? I ask you!"

Every summer, Mr. Shields let us stay at his cabin on Bednesti Lake for exactly one week. It was the highlight of my summer. We had never been to his regular house, but I just knew it would be special.

We pulled up in front of an expansive lawn with bushes and a winding path up to a two story white house with black shutters. *I knew it!* I thought. I had always wanted to live in a house on Patricia Boulevard instead of on the last street in the city. Dad gave me the key while he got a couple of bags from the trunk, and Mom got my brothers out of the back seat. I headed straight to the French doors at the back. They opened onto a wonderful garden: more grass, a bed of red and pink roses, fragrant, multi-coloured sweet peas that climbed the white fence surrounding the garden.

I never wanted to go home again!

I had Bobby's bedroom. The sun streamed through the large window that overlooked the back garden. The single bed, up against one wall, was covered with a brilliantly white bedspread. On one wall, there was a poster of guys playing soccer, on another wall, a poster celebrating a Porsche that had won a race in Mexico. I remembered my dingy little room and its single poster of Cary Grant and Debra Kerr in *An Affair to Remember*. When my friends came over, they always thought that it was there because of Cary Grant.

As I looked around my eyes were drawn to the dresser, and I noticed a framed picture of a woman in her forties. Standing next to the picture, there was a hockey trophy and a ring. It was a class ring of 1957, gold with a large blue stone. I looked into the stone and knew it held the answer. It wouldn't change the past. It might change my future.

I picked up the ring and slipped it on my finger. It was too big, but I knew that all I needed to do was to wind tape around the back. The next day, as soon as I was out of the house, I slipped the ring on my finger.

Before going through the door of the school, I took the ring off and carefully put it into my pencil case. All morning, I kept touching it. I hoped it wouldn't spontaneously combust. Why didn't my school uniform have a pocket? Glancing around, I moved the ring to my lunch box. Would I have the nerve to put it on at lunch?

When lunch was over, I put the ring on my finger and hid my hand behind my back.

"What are you hiding?" Amy asked. Tentatively, I brought my hand out and showed them the ring.

"Where did you get that?"

"Whose is it?"

They were all talking at once.

"Well," I stammered, "I was keeping it secret, but you guys are always talking about boys, and I could never join in. So now here. It's my boyfriend's high school ring. He's away in Toronto at University."

My hands were shaking. Would I get away with it?

Would I be able to get away with the real secret?

All Girls Can Have Curls

Judy Fletcher

A few months into my first year of high school, my mother decides that I need a new look, one that will get the attention of the boys. The transformation begins. She wraps elastic bands round each of the braids that I have worn since I was six, and then she cuts them off. She lays them in a box lined with pink tissue paper. Mom may have seen this touching ritual in a movie or on TV. Almost immediately, the box is misplaced and the braids are never seen again.

The Toni television and magazine ads feature a pair of perky teens in matching sweater sets, no Clearasil for these squeaky clean sisters. They are blondes with soft waves of curls, framing their delicate features and glowing complexions. My mousy brown hair is pulled away from my flat Irish face, which is always covered in freckles and occasionally visited by outbreaks of acne. Toni Home Permanents are marketed to women who can't afford beauty salon prices. Not only can we not afford such luxuries, we live so far out of town that there isn't a salon for miles.

For the next five years, every two months, my mother cuts a few inches off my straggly hair, thus preparing me for the pathetic ritual to come. Each time she hopes the day will end with me, the little tomboy, looking like one of the sweet cheerful "Toni Twins" or the "Toni Twin's" second cousin on their father's side. The whole family hope so too.

Shorn like a sacrificial lamb, I wrap myself in a plastic cape to protect my favourite blue jeans and one of my brother Tommy's cast-off T-shirts. The misery begins with a thorough review of the ten-page instruction booklet. I study this as if my life depends on it. Somewhere in it, I want to find the key to avoiding another hair disaster. My mother, her grey hair too thin to hold a curl, is also wrapped in plastic and wears huge yellow rubber gloves.

She lays out the equipment as I recite from the instruction book.

The most difficult part of home perms is also the most important. Learning how to section and block your hair so that each part has a uniform thickness can be a little tricky, so take your time and practice to avoid an uneven look.

"Yes, yes, I know how to do it," she barks at me.

She begins by combing a few hairs in to a single layer, folds an end paper around it and wraps it around a plastic rod. She snaps it shut against my scalp.

"Ouch, Mom, it says: don't pull the hair too tight or you'll damage it."

On and on it goes for what seems like hours. Some of the curlers refuse to stay where they're put. They pop open, expelling the hair and soggy tissue and bringing forth a steam of unusually colourful language from my mother. Eventually, the successes outnumber the malicious pop-opens and we finish off using cut-up newspaper as replacement for the mound of tissue pulp on the kitchen floor.

We have stopped talking some time ago.

I dare not tell her that the different coloured rods are different sizes and they should follow the pattern in the booklet. Even though my head is covered with these plastic sticks, my mother jams in a few more of the small ones for good measure. My eyes are watering. Our plastic capes are in tatters, and we're both soaked.

According to the booklet, the solution will break down and retrain my hair.

I think of my braids, tidy in their little coffin, whereabouts unknown. I pray that the chemical dousing will work some miracle on what is left of my hair.

Once all of your hair is rolled up, thoroughly saturate every curl with the perm solution. Use all of the solution. Perm processing times are extremely important, so don't get distracted. Never, ever, leave the solution on longer than specified in the instructions. You won't get more curls. You'll get frizz, or worse, your hair could break off or dissolve into a gummy mess.

My mother applies the solution, starting at the back. Within seconds, the stinging liquid runs into my ears and down inside Tommy's T-shirt. I try desperately to keep it out of my eyes with a wadded up facecloth.

After it's done, I wrap myself in a dry towel. We set a kitchen timer and watch the clock. And silently we both pray. I steal a look to see if my mother has her rosary beads in hand. I wonder if there are special prayers for curly hair.

The timer rings and my mother pours gallons of water over me to remove the perm solution. I am wet from head to toe, but we are headed into the home stretch.

Apply the neutralizer. This solution begins the process of re-forming the broken proteins in your hair.

I don't see how this awful smelling stuff can repair anything. It produces enough ammonia to euthanize an elephant if an elephant were to be so foolish as to want kinky hair to go to the school dance in hopes of attracting a mate.

A family of skunks sits on the porch staring in our window.

My mother uses both hands to unlock hundreds of curlers and hurls them towards the sink. Some of them actually land there. Most of the end papers land on the floor.

There is nothing more to do.

Consummatum est.

We march slowly towards the bathroom mirror.

Forlornly staring back at us is a Little Orphan Annie look-alike, only sadder, much sadder.

Silently we clean up the kitchen.

I wonder if this is a good time to tell her that I don't like boys anyways.

Homosexual Suicide

Douglas Bacon

I was sitting at the kitchen table eating a bologna sandwich for lunch, but my mother wasn't talking to me like she usually did when I came home from school. Instead, she was sitting across the table reading the newspaper my father had left from breakfast. He liked reading the news, and sometimes he talked with me about it. My mother hardly ever read the newspaper so I wondered what had got her attention.

I looked at the headlines. The words were upside down, but I could still read them: "Suez Crisis Resolved by Pearson" was at the top of the page, but that wasn't what she was reading. She was looking at something near the bottom of the page. When I saw its heading, I froze – "Homosexual Suicide".

Oh dear God! Oh sweet Jesus! Help me! Help me please!

I didn't know the first word, but I sure knew the second. I knew what suicide was. My mother had tried to suicide the year before, in 1955, when I was nine. I'd come home from school and found her lying flat on the floor of the front hall of our house. I'd called my father at the store, and he'd said he'd called an ambulance.

"Be strong, Dougie," he said. "Be strong." Then he hung up.

When I heard the ambulance siren getting close, I'd got really scared. I guessed my mother was dead. The siren stopped. I opened the front door and saw two men running up the sidewalk carrying a stretcher. They were all dressed in white. Even their shoes were white. When they came in, they sort of nodded at me but didn't say anything. Then they lifted my mother's body onto the gurney, wheeled it outside, and put it in the back of the ambulance.

One of the men came back and said, "You better come with me, son." He put me in the front seat beside the driver and said, "I'll stay in the back with your Mommy." I didn't call her that, but it made me feel better when he said it.

When we got to the hospital, they wheeled my mother inside through double green doors that had a sign over them that said *Emergency Staff Only*. After a while, the ambulance man came back out of the green doors and saw me standing there alone.

He pointed to a bench opposite the doors and said, "You'd better wait there." Then he left. I was alone. I wasn't as scared as before, but the longer I sat waiting, the more upset I got. Why was I the only one who couldn't go through the green doors? I'd gotten Mother to the hospital. Why couldn't I be with her? It wasn't fair. I wanted to run away. But I knew I had to stay.

After what seemed like a long time, my father arrived and sat beside me on the long oak bench that faced the green doors. He reached over and took my hand. He'd never done that before - except for when he taught me to say my prayers. We waited and waited and hardly said anything. Finally the doctor came out.

"She's going to be alright." We both let out a big sigh. Then my father said, "Thank you," to the doctor. On the way home I asked my father what had happened.

"Your mother..." he hesitated. "Your mother attempted suicide, Dougie." I looked at him, but he didn't look at me. He kept looking down.

"What's 'attempted suicide' mean, Daddy?" I asked.

Silence.

Finally, he looked up and said, "She tried to kill herself, Dougie." I saw his tears. Then, he turned away. I was in shock. My mother almost died. And my father had cried. Died. Cried. I'd never seen either before.

That was the day I learned what 'suicide' meant.

All the horror and fears of that night rushed over me when I saw *my mother* reading about 'suicide' in the paper. But beside it was another word that I didn't know, 'homosexual'. The headline said "Homosexual Suicide." I'd never seen that word before. I memorized the spelling so I could look it up in the dictionary: h-o-m-o-s-e-x-u-a-l.

As I was doing that, mother looked up and saw me reading the words.

"Don't read that!" she said. She folded the paper, walked straight to the woodstove, lifted the front plate, shoved in the paper in and watched 'til it caught fire. "Faggots" I heard her mumble. I'd heard her say that word before, usually about some men who were sort of different, but who I thought were handsome, like the men ballet dancers on TV on *The Ed Sullivan Show*.

I knew then that in my mother's mind there was something bad and shameful about the words I'd seen, something a ten year old boy shouldn't know about, something that had to be destroyed. She knew why. I didn't. But I planned to find out as soon as I could!

I finished my lunch, left the house, and ran the three blocks to Queen Alexandra School. I was in Grade Six and, like every student, I had a *Nelson's Highroads Dictionary* in my desk. I searched for the word: 'homosexual.'

Where was it? I found the word 'homonym' but the next word was 'honour' with a 'u'. It wasn't there.

I decided I'd have to look it up in the dictionary my older brother had won for standing first in English in Grade Twelve in 1950. He kept it in his bookcase in his room. When I got home and opened *The Concise Oxford Dictionary of Current English*, I looked. And I looked again... and again. I couldn't find it. There were several words I'd never seen before, but this time there was nothing between 'homoousian' and 'homunculus'.

I was getting really curious now. Why wasn't the word 'homosexual' in the dictionary? I decided I'd be like the Hardy Boys and be a kid on a detective search, so the next day I went to the main branch of the Peterborough Public Library, convinced there had to be a dictionary there that would have the word. I asked the librarian to show me where the biggest dictionaries were. When I told her that I'd already looked at *The Concise Oxford Dictionary* I think she was impressed, because she opened her eyes wide, smiled at me and nodded her head. We walked to the Reference Room and she took down six big dictionaries from an upper shelf. Two of them were humungous! I thanked her then got to work. This is what I found:

In *Webster's Giant Illustrated Dictionary*, 'homorganic' was followed by 'homoteria'.1

In *Merriam-Webster's The Academic Dictionary of the English Language* 'homonymous' was followed by 'homotenous'.2

In *The Oxford English Dictionary, Vol.5 H-K,* 'homopterous' was followed by 'homostyled'.3

In the *Thorndike-Barnhart Dictionary,* 'homo sapiens' was followed by 'Honduras'.4

In *Macmillan's Modern Dictionary of the English Language,* 'homoncule' was followed by 'Hon'.5

And in *Funk & Wagnall's Standard Dictionary of the English Language,* 'homoptera' was followed by 'homotaxis'.6

I'd seen a lot of words I'd never seen before, but still hadn't found 'homosexual'. Puzzled and disappointed, I left the library and headed home.

As I walked up George Street past my church and some of my friends' houses, I thought maybe the newspaper had invented the word, but I doubted it. Robertson Davies was the editor and publisher of *The Peterborough Examiner.* My Grade Six teacher, Mr. Dawson, and my father often said Mr. Davies was brilliant, so I knew he knew a lot about words and wouldn't just make up a word that didn't mean anything. Then, I figured I might ask my father what the word meant. He'd told me the meaning of 'suicide' so maybe he'd tell me the meaning of 'homosexual'. But not in front of mother, he wouldn't. I'd have to wait and ask him on the weekend. That would give me time to think about it some more.

Yes. I'd have to think more about it before I asked, before I asked my father, or well, before I asked anybody.

****

1. *homorganic*: pronounced by the same vocal organs' *homoteria*: a kind of cafeteria where patrons serve themselves
2. *homonymous*: equivocal, ambiguous; *homotenous*: equable, of equal tenor
3. *homopterous*: belonging to or having the characters of the Homoptera; *homostyled*: having the styles or pistilis…of the same length relative to the stamens

4. *homo sapiens*: modern man; *Honduras*: a country in Central America

5. *homoncule*: little man, dwarf; *Hon.*: Honourable (as son of a peer)

6. *Homoptera*: a subspecies of hemipterous insects; *homotaxis:* similarity of strata determined primarily by fossils

Love in Montreal

Greta Hurst

It was June 1957, and I had just completed the retail course at Sir George Williams College. Lorrie was one of the salespeople in the sportswear boutique at Montreal's smallest department store, Ogilvy's. She was the youngest and friendliest of all the staff. Eight years older than me, she was unlike anyone I had ever met. She wore pants, a plain shirt, and no make-up to work - unusual for women in Montreal. The other saleswomen came to work wearing dressy clothes with scarves, earrings, and full makeup - as if they were going to a party afterwards.

She invited me home to dinner. She lived with her husband in a small house near the top of the hill in Westmount, a treed street in one of Montreal's upscale neighbourhoods. Nick greeted me at the door of an ordinary house; conventional furniture, somber in colour, it seemed to reflect Nick's personality. Lorrie came out of the kitchen. She had prepared one of my favourite meals - roast lamb and eggplant.

As the three of us sat around the square dining room table, I thought Nick could have been Lorrie's brother; their personalities were so similar. They asked me lots of questions about my life and interests. Oh, I was full of myself! I told them about going every weekend to the country cabin in the Laurentians. I bragged about getting a B+ in my course. I didn't tell them about shoveling snowdrifts and freezing weather, nor that I failed 10th grade miserably. I didn't mention living in a rundown, working class neighbourhood near the Main. I didn't tell them that until recently, I had been shy and introverted.

Montreal was the biggest, most cosmopolitan city in Canada. It was a fun-loving, jazz-crazy city with nightclubs that welcomed Afro-American musicians who were not able to perform in the US. I tried to persuade them to come and see Oscar Peterson, who was playing at one of the clubs, but Nick said they never went out in the evening.

One evening Nick went off to a meeting. We were cleaning up after dinner when Lorrie suggested continuing our conversation about sex.

"Come sit on the sofa with me." She motioned me to sit beside her.

When I sat, she went on, "Have you ever kissed a woman? Would you like to try?"

Always game for anything new and possibly exciting, I moved towards her. She kissed me slowly. It was soft, tender and long. "We have lots of time before he comes home," she said while her hands moved over my body. The hair on my arms stood up and blood raced through my body as she kissed my face and caressed my breasts. We became lovers.

Lorrie wanted to meet my mother - the dragon eater. The night before my mother and I were leaving on a trip, Lorrie turned up to help me pack. The next day she came to say goodbye, wearing a skirt and high-heeled shoes. My mother hated her on sight.

In that steely-eyed way of hers, she asked me, "Why did she come here?" I decided not to answer.

I called my mother on my morning break when I knew she'd be up. I didn't know why, but she did. She came straight to the point. "Either stop seeing Lorrie or you have to leave home." My sister had betrayed me.

I moved in with Lorrie and Nick. My sister fed the firestorm by telling our mutual friends. Overnight, I was ostracized; I felt like a leper, a social outcast. Lorrie and I didn't know any gay people. As she didn't want her husband to know the truth, she rented an apartment where we'd have privacy - a love nest with only a mattress on the bedroom floor and a bare light bulb.

That year passed in a blur. While Lorrie continued to work at Ogilvy's, I found another job. We didn't go out nor make any friends. I wanted Lorrie to divorce Nick. She did. But it didn't make any difference. Less than a year later, Lorrie showed me a ticket. She was returning to her family home in Europe.

"Why can't I come with you?" I despaired. She had asked her parents but they refused. I didn't hear from Lorrie again.

****

By January 1977, I was married, with three children under 10, and about to celebrate my 41st birthday. We had moved to Europe in 1973, going to north Germany for a year before moving to Brussels in June 1974. In Brussels, I joined an English-language feminist group, *The Women's Organization for Equality*. At the first meeting I attended, I stood at the back of the room, terrified. Listening to Lydia, *WOE's* matriarch, I realized I'd either have to leave the meeting immediately or my life would be changed beyond recognition. I stayed, but it took me two years in consciousness-raising groups to fully understand the politics of being a wife and mother.

When our group hosted the March 1976 International Tribunal of Crimes Against Women, 2,000 women attended. Speakers testified about the living conditions of women in their countries. Irish women told that birth control was illegal in Ireland. Abortion was still illegal everywhere, but marital rape was legal, not recognized as a crime. Lesbians from the United States reported being told not to discuss their issues in the *National Organization for Women* as heterosexual women would be upset - afraid people would think them lesbians. In most countries, lesbians didn't reveal their sexual identities to avoid rape by men trying to *re-educate* them. Women could be imprisoned and murdered for being lesbian. On day one, two hundred lesbians from Berlin protested the fact that lesbian issues were scheduled to be discussed only on the last day. The agenda was quickly changed.

For me, the political became personal on a romantic level when I met Nicole, a member of our group. In January 1977, I came out as a lesbian. It was easily the most painful experience of my life. I left my children with their father and a babysitter. I moved into my own apartment. I wish I could have done it differently.

Flight

Chris Spencer

Miss Roscoe placed the record on the gramophone. As the music started, Kit gazed out of the open windows, across the lawn to the lake. The grass was hazy with heat. A couple of swans were courting, gracefully touching, near touching, then caressing, and it struck Kit that this was exactly how she would like to be with Val of the lower sixth. This must be what others called a *crush*. It felt strange, scary and new all at once. What could be done? Kit's instinct told her to keep quiet until she'd figured out the next step. Until then, she could dream on.

The morning hadn't started out too well.

A cigarette had hung on Hilda's lip as she stirred the porridge. Intent on sharing her frustrations she shouted, "You're not fit to live with! Nobody will ever love you. You don't deserve it"

Kit flinched as her mother's fury lashed her; the lump in her throat got tighter and tighter, so that she couldn't have spoken even if she'd wanted to. Unable to disguise her feeling in her eyes and face, she had nowhere to hide. She looked down at her porridge.

There was a knock at the door. It was Val calling on her way to the bus stop.

Hilda opened the door, "Hello Val. Chris won't be a minute- she's just finishing breakfast. How's your mother? Keeping well, I hope? After all she's been through…"

Val said, "Yes, she's doing very well now. Thanks for asking, Mrs. Nicholls."

As they walked to the bus stop, Val asked her "Are you OK, Kit?"

Kit forced the words over the lump in her throat... "Not really, but I don't want to talk about it."

She watched Val's face carefully for any gesture or expression of understanding. There was no such sign. Kit concentrated on the pavement and kept on breathing, praying for the bus to come quickly.

The music of Dvorak wrapped around her: it felt as if she'd flown to a far off country where there was lots of space and very few people. She envisaged rolling plains and high mountains. This was a long way from Buddy Holly or Frankie Vaughan. Miss Roscoe beamed at Kit, as if to share a love for the music. In order to throw Miss Roscoe off the scent, Kit tilted her head in imitation of the HMV dog, and the Rozzer moved on, disappointed. As Kit slowly engaged with Latin declensions and algebra, her anxiety retreated. It finally disappeared in the crucible of Miss Roscoe's dismay.

Kit stopped tilting back in her chair. The next movement in the symphony had started. She saw herself nestled in between the wings, hanging on to the back of one of the swans, away from the present. Val could come with her if she wished. The swan's shoulders would be strong enough for two.

About the 1960s and 1970s

Elise Chenier

The 60s and 70s are probably the most stereotyped decades of the twentieth century. In Canada and the United States, baby boomers came of age and launched a serious challenge to the status quo. JFK and Pierre Trudeau will forever be the iconic leaders of the era, representing the hopes and dreams of the "new" generation, but politicians could never, or would never, go far enough to achieve the systemic change Yippies, sexual and women's liberationists, anti-war activists, the Black Panthers, and the Front de Liberation du Quebec called for.

To understand the roots of this period of radical protest, we must look to the American civil rights movement of the 1950s, for it was this movement, led by Martin Luther King Jr. and soldiered by tens of thousands of Americans of all ages and many racial and ethnic heritages, that laid the groundwork and provided much of the inspiration for the movements of the 1960s and early 70s.

When African-Americans went off to war in the early 1940s, they and their loved ones often held up their index and middle finger on both hands in support of their service. What in the late 60s came to be known as the peace sign was in the 40s known as the V for Victory sign. African-Americans held up both hands in the V form to signify a wish for two victories: victory over fascism in Europe and victory over racism in America. At war's end, racial segregation was challenged, but it took the Montgomery bus boycott, launched in 1955 by Rosa Parks and led by Reverend Martin Luther King Jr., to ignite a national mass movement that renewed energy among blacks who sought change through community and political action, and elevated white America's consciousness about the racial divide.

Young white students in the American northeast were devastated to learn that "America, the land of freedom and opportunity," was more myth than reality. "We are people of this generation, bred in at least modest comfort, housed now in universities, looking uncomfortably to the world we inherit," began the 1962 manifesto of the Students for a Democratic Society (SDS). They challenged the "Establishment's" complicity in the systemic inequality the civil rights movement had so effectively illuminated. Two important SDS legacies are the mass mobilization of youth to fight racial injustice and empower African Americans and the adoption of the politics of empowerment. They ceded leadership to African Americans, they advanced no single economic or political theory, focusing instead on social justice. They rejected hierarchical leadership structures in favour of collectives and collaboration. The subsequent anti-Vietnam war movement was in many respects an extension of the civil rights movement and the work of the SDS. It built on the energy of youth and strategies of political protest hammered out in the civil rights and student movements.

Sexism and homophobia in both movements, however, drove women and lesbians and gays to form their own organizations, organizations that were committed to liberating society from the constraints of sex and gender norms. For women who were not heterosexual, a dilemma emerged. Many found that gay liberation groups were male dominated and plagued by sexist attitudes. Women's liberation organizations, on the other hand, were often homophobic, or at the very least concerned that openly lesbian members were a public relations disaster.

For those who became politically active, hiding one's sexuality was not an option. Lesbians, gays, and other sex and gender non-conformists regarded coming out as one of the most potent revolutionary strategies for challenging homophobia and asserting the human right to sexual freedom and dignity. This direct action model of confronting social attitudes was dramatically illustrated at the second Congress to Unite Women in New York. Lesbians challenged their exclusion from the Congress program and protested disparaging comments about lesbians made by Betty Friedan, founder of the *National Organization for Women* (NOW). Wearing T-shirts emblazoned with the words "Lavender Menace," seventeen-plus activists staged a "zap." Using humor and non-violent confrontation they challenged delegates to confront homophobia in the women's movement and distributed the now famous manifesto, "The Woman-Identified Woman." Although it did not end homophobia in the women's movement, it did create a space for dialogue. Lesbians in Canada were similarly silenced within feminist organizations, including the *National Committee for the Status of Women*.

Gay men and lesbians did occasionally collaborate, sometimes with great success. One example is the Canadian gay liberation newspaper, *The Body Politic*. Editorial board members Gerald Hannon, Rick Bébout, and Ed Jackson were joined by important female contributors such as writer and activist Jane Rule and Chris Bearchell. Well known in this era is the highly public confrontation at the 1973 meeting of the *American Psychiatric Association*. Here both men and women worked collaboratively both behind the scenes and on the front lines to challenge the APA's classification of homosexuality as a mental disease. Their actions were successful and the Association's membership voted to remove it from the *Diagnostic Statistical Manual*. As the decade progressed and activism turned toward pressuring local, state and provincial governments to enact non-discrimination laws and by-laws, lesbians and gay men collaborated more and more frequently toward these initiatives.

Given the centrality of the civil rights movement in inspiring and shaping the protest movements of the 1960s, it is a bitter irony that in both Canada and the US, people of white heritage dominated the women's and gay liberation movements. This is not because people of colour were disinterested in the emerging political scene. Nor was it only a matter of overt racism on the part of white people. The notion of liberation and even gay and feminist identity that defined these movements was often based on a white worldview. When women of colour challenged that worldview, particularly the claim that sexism overrides all other forms of oppression, they were seen as not "real" feminists. The experiences of people of colour in gay activism were similar. For example, gay liberationists regarded the family as an oppressive, bourgeois structure that contributed directly to sexual oppression. This was in direct conflict with the perspectives of people of colour for whom the family, and, in some cases, the church provided essential refuge from racism and was the source of emotional and psychic sustenance. For indigenous people in Canada, it was the genocidal practices of colonizing governments that robbed them of family, and by extension, their language, political systems, and culture, that was at the root of their oppression.

People of colour also experienced racism in the burgeoning cultural scene. Predominantly white bar-goers viewed people of non-white heritage through a racialized lens. Asian men were eroticized as passive and submissive, African men as aggressive and dominant. Women experienced similar forms of marginalization and exoticization. Just as white women and lesbians and gays left civil rights and anti-war movements because of entrenched sexism and homophobia, many people of colour struck out on their own and formed communities of support, networking, and political activism. The mid-1960s formation of Salsa Soul Sisters in New York City was a very early example of this. By the late 1980s, there were many organizations serving diverse populations, though of course most were located in large urban centres.

Lesbian and gay culture also exploded in this period. Bars, dance clubs and bathhouses served people's desire to get out and meet others, to "let your hair down," "shake your booty," and "push, push in the bush." New lesbian and gay bookstores such as *Glad Day Bookstore* in Toronto, *Little Sisters* in Vancouver, *A Different Light* in San Francisco and *Oscar Wilde's* in New York City popped up in most major cities. Here one could find all manner of publications, from books and 'zines to new magazines like the *Advocate* and *Kinesis*, to the gay liberationist paper *The Body Politic*. Papering the walls were announcements about dances, art shows, discussion groups, support groups, book clubs, political rallies - you name it. Book reading may be a solitary activity, but bookstores were an important place to connect. Standing and staring at those posters and fingering the pages of newly discovered books was for many the equivalent to ponying up to a bar and cradling a bottle of beer.

A lesbian and gay arts scene also expanded in this decade. Key was the creation of gay and lesbian-run spaces, and the emergence of events promoters who catered to this niche market. These developments enabled musicians and artists to be *out*, to address lesbian and gay themes and issues, and have an audience with whom to engage. The Michigan Womyn's Music Festival, established in 1976, encouraged the development of new talent. Other performers like the Village People were able to appeal to a gay audience and still enjoyed mainstream success, although they, like Freddie Mercury of Queen, remained in the closet. Lesbian and gay theatre and other arts organizations emerged alongside the music scene. All of these groups, including the people that published and promoted these works, typically worked out of small, non-profit spaces for low or no wages.

Trans people were also beginning to "come out." In the 1950s, ex-GI Christine Jorgenson had attracted an extraordinary amount of media attention for her gender transition, and Dr. Harry Benjamin emerged in the same decade as a leading advocate for trans rights. Judy Bowen formed *Transsexuals and Transvestites* in New York. Reed Erickson's *Educational Foundation*, established in the 1960s and supported by his personal wealth, provided critical funding for transsexual research. Ariadne Kane filled a need for a gathering place for trans people in the early 1970s. She coordinated three *New England Conferences on Alternate Sex and Gender Lifestyles* and organized *Fantasia Fair* in Provincetown, a gathering that continues to the present day.

Hollywood took an interest in transsexual and transgender experience, although it was sometimes packaged as "gay" cinema. Gore Vidal's satirical novel *Myra Breckenridge* was made into a feature film in 1970. Two years later, Toronto playwright John Herbert's *Fortune and Men's Eyes*, first staged off-off Broadway in 1968, was made into an MGM feature. The 1972 feature *Dog Day Afternoon* recounted the real-life experience of John Wojtowicz and Sal Naturale who attempted to rob the Chase Manhattan Bank in Brooklyn to get money for Wojtowicz's lover's sex change operation. For some people, filmic representations such as these were a welcome relief from the deafening silence that surrounded queer desire and queer life. These films are also a testament to the fascination with genderqueer lives in the early 1970s, but they appear as *freaks*, not as everyday people. Though important, these films did not significantly ease the social censure trans people experienced.

By the mid-1970s, lesbians and gays of white heritage appeared to be on the cusp of making very real social and political gains. Pressure to adopt anti-discrimination ordinances in the US and to entrench sexual orientation in human rights codes in Canada was winning over politicians and the public. Anti-discrimination measures were easy to grasp since they were based on similar initiatives advanced by the civil rights movement. These developments, however, caught the attention of conservative forces. In Florida, former Miss America contestant Anita Bryant was recruited to represent Christian opposition to the anti-discrimination ordinance passed in Dade County. In the second half of the 1970s, she, along with Christian televangelist Jerry Falwell, became the face of the *moral majority*. A coalition of morally conservative Christian forces opposed the liberalization of sexual mores and laws. Bryant's campaign to repeal such ordinances enjoyed some success, and Canadian evangelists invited her north to share her message.

Bryant's campaign mobilized her opponents, too, and her public appearances become the target for gay rights activists. Once again, gay men and lesbians worked together to oppose a common enemy. The conflict provided colourful material for the media, especially as one of the protest tactics popular at the time was to "pie" the offending party. Many lesbians and gays viewed photographs of Anita Bryant's face smothered in cream pie with delight.

Bryant's campaign, however, was only a minor skirmish in the much bigger war to win control the reigns of political power in the United States. Whereas Canada's conservative factions remained liberal and sometimes even progressive on social and sexual issues until the 2000s, the American religious right aggressively campaigned to transform political life by attacking sexual and social liberalism, including women's and gay rights. By the mid-1970s, the gay liberation movement had lost a lot of steam; the rise of the religious right prompted new forms of protest and organized opposition. The lesbian and gay music and theatre scene, the newspapers, the bookstores, and even the bathhouses all played a role in increasing awareness of the new political assault on gay and lesbian life, and were recruiting grounds for new political activists.

As the stories in this section show, however, it was personal connections that helped people cross the bridge from normativity to queer life. Few ventured into a bar or a community dance on their own. As Pat Hogan's story eloquently shows, people already living out and proud lives were sources of inspiration and anxiety: that's who I wish I were, but I could never be that. They provided road maps for how to re-imagine life outside of the mainstream. This is the role that stories have always played, including coming out stories. By reading them, we learn how to give expression to our desires, how to dress, to communicate, and even how to make love. Sandra Mudd's story shows us an alternative to the alternative. Not everyone was attracted to the *scene*. What came to define lesbian and gay life – Judy Garland, drag shows, and heavy drinking in second-rate bars that tolerated *queers* -- was as unappealing as marriage, children, and laundry.

For gay men in particular, the 1970s were about to become a "golden era." At the end of the decade, signs of a strange but deadly illness spreading among the community were emerging, leading to widespread panic and confusion, and most of all, profound loss and sadness, as Chris Mann's deeply touching story illustrates. What eventually came to be known as Acquired Immune Deficiency Syndrome (AIDS) would, in the decade to come, radically transform the community and its politics and culture. And once again lesbians and gay men, and increasingly trans folk, would come together to mourn their losses and to struggle for a better future.

Shock!

Val Innes

SHOCK

VAL INNES

IT WAS 1971, AND JENNIE AND HER GIRLFRIEND, DEB, WERE 16 AND LOVERS, EAGER TO HAVE ANY CHANCE TO BE ALONE TOGETHER.

A SLEEPOVER WAS A TREAT, AND THIS TIME, JENNIE'S PARENTS WERE OUT FOR THE EVENING.

BUT THEY WERE TOO LOST IN EACH OTHER TO PAY ATTENTION TO THE TIME . . .

AND ALL HELL BROKE LOOSE . . .

THAT'S DISGUSTING, JENNIE. YOU'RE SICK. I'M SENDING YOU TO THE PSYCH WARD! THEY'LL FIX YOU!

Veiled

Christine Waymark

The new church is on the opposite corner from where our old one stood. It's a large white building with big oak doors. In 1961, *new* for the United Church of Canada means straight lines and blonde wood. The windows are tall and narrow, with stained glass in an angular design. Inside, a plain silver cross hangs by a chain from a narrow steeple set into a circle of skylights. The electric organ and the choir stall face the pulpit rather than the congregation. The only colour is the blue carpet down the central aisle.

I'm 20 and the first bride to go down this aisle. We wait next to the sanctuary door. Mother confiscated my glasses, so I see a blur. Under my homemade gown, I wear a borrowed crinoline, which keeps me from standing close to anyone. On my thigh is the blue garter mum wore on her wedding day.

My veil is a circle of net with a deep lace edging. I wear it folded into two and gathered into the headdress mum thought might make me look taller.

I don't like it.

Five bridesmaids line up behind me in the English tradition. Made from the same pattern, the long dresses are the newest fashion of flocked nylon over taffeta. The maid of honour wears lavender, followed by two friends in pink and two small flower girls proud in blue. Mum made matching headdresses and fingerless gloves for them all.

I long for the old church. The mahogany pews shone with the buffing of many generations. It was easy to sing out favourite hymns to the music from the gold pipes behind the tiered choir loft. The carved oak pulpit cradled an ancient leather Bible. The deep maroon carpet matched the gowns of the choir. One Sunday, looking down from my place in the teen choir, I'd noticed bobbing and sliding on the pew. As Jean dropped down to the floor, the minister stopped his sermon. "We'll wait until young Jean is back with us," he said gently. Red-faced, she emerged with her shoe in hand. Many of us laughed along with her friend, Robin.

They are here today at my wedding. Jean, a tall slender athletic teen, will walk this same aisle in five years to marry my brother. Curly haired Robin, who has a big smile and a beautiful voice, will take a different route.

It's time.

Mum bustles up and drapes half of the veil over my face, kissing me on the cheek as she does it. Now what I see is even blurrier. The mother of the bride marches down the aisle. I take Dad's arm to go into the sanctuary. As the organist strikes the first chords of "Here Comes the Bride," Dad says quietly, "It's not too late to go the other way."

"Keep walking" I hiss, and we turn for the long walk past the decorated pews, filled with family and friends, to the altar where the men wait. I am about to become Mrs. Reginald Partridge.

I try to look around, but I can't make out who I'm looking at and feel a little queasy as I try. So I look straight into the blur in front of me. The music seeps into my consciousness, and with the words *big, fat, and wide* ringing in my mind, I remember that I asked not to have this music. I dismiss the thought that no one ever listens to me.

I walk with purpose towards the man I have chosen. I know his face well, and my brain fills in what my eyes can't see. I love his dark, curly hair and blue eyes that show his Celtic ancestry. We talk politics and religion. He is artistic and loves Jazz. He is gentle and loving with my four-year-old sister, missing his own teenage sister who still lives in England.

Reverend Kennedy begins the well-known words. "We are gathered together..."

I am getting married.

We promise to love honour and cherish, until death do us part. I'm modern enough that I don't promise to obey. Reg lifts my veil, placing it gently over my headdress and hair. My eyes have grown more accustomed to seeing, and as we turn to face the congregation, I look at my church full of family, friends and feel the warmth of their support.

I tuck my arm into Reg's, and we stride forward into what I believe will be the rest of my life.

Before I Knew the Word

Pat Hogan

Monday through Friday, I drive my red '53 Chevrolet convertible from home to Danville (pop. 800) where I work in the traffic department office at the factory, located right where the railroad tracks intersect Route 101 heading south to Rhode Island and north to Hartford. I fill out bills of lading and take notes for my boss in shorthand.

It's not an interesting job; in fact, it's boring. But, I have to start someplace, and this was the best I can find after high school. $57 a week is not to be sneezed at.

Mr. Mercier, my boss, doesn't speak to me much anymore. This is not unusual here in the traffic department. The people who work on the floor have worked side by side for years, filling orders and packing boxes of *sewing notions*, which are shipped all around the world. They punch in at the time clock in the morning, punch out at night, often working in a dead silence that can, and does, continue for months, even years.

No one knows anymore what caused these silences, why no one utters even a "good morning" to their co-workers standing across the packing table. It's just the way it is. Their lives go on, day in, day out. They do their work, take two coffee breaks - one in the morning, one in afternoon - either out on the platform where the freight is loaded onto trucks or in a dingy little bathroom downstairs. They have their lunch break, go home at night, return the next morning, and pick up their paychecks at the end of the month. It's life in The Quiet Corner.

Bob Wielder, the floor supervisor, isn't much help in easing the daily tensions. His rigid smile and body says it all. He too fears Mercier, and his job is at stake. At the top of the factory hierarchy is Mr. Posner himself. He shows up unannounced in our department on occasion, always wearing a pinstriped suit, white shirt, and tie. A tall and straight-backed man in his 50's, he peers around the department through thick, round-rim glasses, his thinning hair parted in the middle and slicked down on the sides. His darting eyes and grunts as he examines the work put us on edge; if only he would smile once in awhile. But, his face is waxen, expressionless. When he does speak, in his thick German accent, it's only to Bob or Mercier. On these visits, the usual tension in the traffic department expands and permeates the floor. It's agonizing.

When Mercier does speak to me, it's usually one liners like "What's the sluice, kid?" - his morning greeting (if he's in a good mood, that is) as he passes my desk on his way to his office, eyes averted, looking straight ahead.

One day stands out from all the rest. I get a call from Head Office. Someone wants to see me, I'm told.

Head office is at the opposite end of the building from the traffic department. Like most New England mills, the factory rambles on, spread out over several blocks. The clicking of my high heels echoes along the narrow passageway - a long wooden dusty floor with high stacks of packed cartons on either side.

I click past cartons waiting to be piled onto the trailer trucks that arrive each day at the traffic department's bay. Sewing notions are shipped to fashion designers around the world. *Sewing notions,* I think, inconsequentially. *What a strange term. Why 'notions'?*

I head down a flight of stairs, across another long passageway leading to the main building of the plant, up more stairs and into the waiting room. *Am I getting fired,* I wonder? I'm wearing one of my new Tycora sweater sets – a light blue short sleeve pullover with matching cardigan, and a reversible skirt (the rage) held together mid-calf with a big stylish safety pin. I look good.

Did Mercier get mad the last time I took time off? Or was I late for work one too many times? Am I getting a raise? Many questions whirl through my mind as I take a deep breath, push open the heavy metal door with glass window and walk into the reception room leading to the head office.

The receptionist nods her head towards someone standing in the waiting area. "Visitor for you."

And there, standing in front of me, in dungarees, button-down shirt and sneakers is my friend Carol, looking cute as ever in her tomboyish athletic way, hands on hips, head cocked to one side, grinning. Carol was my first dyke friend, even before I knew the word. She was the ringleader of a gang of girls who were having sex together in high school before they know the word for what they were doing. The school dean, a woman, got in a flutter when she got wind of it. She crept into the girls' room when she knew they'd be in there, and crouched up on a toilet, feet up on the door, to listen. It was juicy, scandalous, unheard of in our high school!

The thing is, despite her escapade with the girls, Carol always had a boyfriend and married soon after high school. The way it went in those days for girls was this: you either went on to college after high school, got a job, or got married, or a combination of all three. The wedding was a big event and four of us from the old gang marched down the aisle in matching salmon taffeta gowns and shoes. It was a typical Catholic wedding, church packed with family and friends from school - we knew everyone there.

Everyone was counting on the reception after the church Mass. A wedding reception meant music, food, dancing, drinking - a party! And a party it was! The bride and groom had the first dance together. We oohed and aahed. At the end of the day, we waved goodbye as they left for a honeymoon and their new home together 100 miles away. The marriage didn't last long - six months to be exact. Actually, it was annulled, and in the Catholic Church, that meant only one thing.

Today Carol doesn't waste words, just looks me straight in the eye and says, "Hey, Pat. I'm hitchhiking to California. Are you coming?"

Me, go to California? Hitchhiking? My jaw dropped.

I stammer, "Well, I...I have to think about it." Carol looks at me, somewhat scornfully, shrugs her shoulders, and leaves. She makes it to California, and we don't see each other for years.

Truth told, I was chicken -- chicken to take off on a whim, chicken to "ask" my mother, chicken to do something out of the ordinary.

Three months later I left my job at the factory. Mercier said nothing when I gave notice, but on my last day of work he came and offered me a gruff, "Good bye and good luck" and shook my hand.

I worked there for three years before heading for New York. The others were there for a lifetime.

First Time's Special

Val Innes

She'd done her homework, as much as she could. She'd done the reading, furtively buying books whenever and wherever she could find them. She'd made the phone call, talked to the gay and lesbian phone line helper, Jennie, and now she was ready. Wasn't she? Well, anyway, here she was. She should fit in pretty well, Jennie said. She had on faded jeans with rolled up cuffs over her boots and a red and black plaid shirt over her T-shirt.

She looked around. Yep. Looked like a dance hall. A bit gritty – old, wooden floor, tables and chairs, dingy green paint on the walls with some ancient nature pictures hanging a bit askew. Sounded like a dance hall. Lots of loud music, talk and laughter. Felt like a dance hall. Had that vibe to it. But, wow, something different, though... Look at all the *women*!

Women dancing together, laughing with each other, hands in the air to *Sisters Are Doin' it for Themselves*, bodies touching, clinging, breaking off to swirl back, hands on hips, flirting, teasing, breasts touching. One couple was doing a great jive to the music, and a whole group was dancing together around them. And at the tables, more women, sitting talking, drinking, smoking - a group near her arguing loudly almost over the music, and over there, a couple of women making out - kissing! And against the bar and the walls, women watching the action, like she was. Some drinking, some just quietly talking, some just propping the wall up, watching. Women everywhere, all over the place.

And here was one woman moving towards *her*!

Mary watched as she came near - tall, attractive, with a tan set off by her white shirt and black jeans, a silver chain around her neck, silver rings on her fingers, short blonde hair swept back and intense blue eyes seeking hers.

"Hi there. I'm Terry. You're new here, aren't you?"

"Yes, I am. New to everything here."

"Ahh... first time?"

"Yes."

"Well, then. Come and dance with me! First time's special. I'd like that. To be special."

Mary paused. Looked at her. Looked at the women dancing. Felt a tingle right down to her toes. And said, "Let's dance!"

And they did.

All the Women

Marsha Ablowitz

Marsha woke up kissing Ran's soft eyebrows, then jolted awake as she realized she was late for the conference. She snuck out of bed, but as she pulled on her raggedy jeans, the phone rang and she tripped over the tangle of its cord. Down it crashed.

"It's nothing Ran. It's for me. I've got to get to the conference."

Marsha stretched the cord out into the hall and closed the bedroom door.

"Hello."

"I just wanted to wish you a happy day at the conference."

"Fuck" thought Marsha. She stared sightlessly at the Black Panther poster on the wall. Without her bidding, an image of Kim's breasts slid into her brain.

"Don't let him know it's me."

"I won't." No time for a scene. "Hey, Kim…how 'bout you come with me? Its gonna be wonderful with all the women."

Kim's voice turned hard. "Marsha, I've told you if you tell anyone about us I will kill myself."

"I'm sorry. Please don't do anything. Don't hurt yourself, Kim. I really love you. But look, I'm late. I've just got to go. I really love you Kim."

Happily singing along with her car radio - "All You Need is Love, Love, Love" -Marsha sped up the 10th Ave. hill to the University of B.C. She was a housing volunteer at the first day of the Women's Vietnam Peace Conference. It was a sunny morning. Rushing up the stairs of the student union, Marsha ran her fingers through her long black hair and remembered she hadn't brushed her teeth. She glanced at the *Peace*

Now and the *Vietnam Woman's Conference* posters plastered on the walls and paused at the poster of the Mai Lai Massacre. Piles of dead bodies, naked, with GI's standing over them, pointing their machine guns at dead women and old people and children. "Those same GIs are dropping napalm on the villages in North Vietnam right now," she thought.

The registration office was full of young American women. They had to come to Canada for the peace conference because the U.S. wouldn't let the North Vietnamese keynote speakers enter the US. Vancouver progressives and Communists had the bright idea to hold a peace conference in Canada, because Canada was not at war with North Viet Nam. Mrs. Baker from the *Voice of Women* organized the conference and invited women's groups from the USA. Marsha thought the *Voice of Women* was a square group of old women, even though they were communists and progressives, but Marsha's cool Women's Lib group had nonetheless decided to volunteer. The Women's Liberation members all wanted to meet the Vietnamese women fighters. Also they hoped to talk a lot with the heroic Black Panther women.

Marsha pulled off her jacket and dropped it on the floor. Mrs. Baker was already organizing the office, and delegates lined the hall wanting billets. Mrs. Baker smiled at Marsha, even though she was late.

"Good you are here, Marsha," she said. "Take these housing lists and give the women their billeting addresses after I register them."

As Marsha pulled up the wooden folding chair and took her seat at the housing registration table, she noticed she had pulled on her worn torn jeans.

Cool.

Mrs. Baker turned back to a thin young woman delegate wearing striped bellbottoms, a fringed leather jacket, and holding a teddy bear.

"Sorry. Your group needs to sleep on the floor."

"O.K. that's cool. We have sleeping bags, and I brought my pillow. I always bring my pillow."

Marsha looked up at the wimpy bellbottomed woman who needed a pillow, and then looked at Mrs. Baker. She didn't look like a communist.

"How's Ran? Is he coming to the conference?" asked Mrs. Baker. She really liked Ran. Everyone did. He was Sensei, 3rd generation Japanese Canadian, so cute and enthusiastic.

"Sure Mrs. Baker, Ran will be here later," said Marsha.

She turned to the next woman in line. She had dark blue eyes and long brown hair with blond sun streaks. She wore a multi colored bandanna round her head and a loose low necked paisley long sleeved blouse over jeans and light brown work boots. Marsha thought maybe she wasn't wearing a bra.

"Hi I'm Jean from Corvallis. I'm representing the Oregon Lesbian Caucus. It was sure good of you Canadian women to organize this conference, so we can meet with the Vietnamese women."

Marsha wondered how Jean could say the word *lesbian* so calmly. If only Kim were here! Maybe meeting Jean would help Kim get over her fears of being found out. Kim's father hated gays.

Just then two tall Black women stomped into the office. They didn't wait for their turn in the line, just pushed in front of the white women. The room was quiet. Quiet.

Jean looked up startled, saw the black women and said, "I'll be back later."

The tall black woman was heavy with strong features. She was wearing dark framed sunglasses, a shiny black jacket and black men's shoes. She had a giant Afro hairdo. Marsha figured the big woman's hair jumped out at least eight inches from the edge of her head. How did she keep her black tam on? The second woman was slighter with a shorter sleeker Afro, an identical black tam, and a black shirt with the picture of a crouching panther. They both moved quickly and decisively, looming over Marsha and Mrs. Baker.

"We are the Black Panthers from Oakland," said the big haired woman. "We need to borrow your guns."

"What?...Guns? Guns...? said Marsha. "Umm...what do you mean?"

"The fucking guards at the border took our guns. We need to protect ourselves. You need to lend us your guns," said the big woman.

"But..but...we don't have any guns. This is Canada, not Oakland," said Marsha.

Marsha was twenty-seven years old and figured she'd seen a lot. But she had only seen black women like this before in *Ramparts Magazine*. The black students on campus were mainly skinny polite foreign students from places like Trinidad and India.

"Aren't guns for freedom fighters in places like Cuba and Vietnam?" she thought quickly. She had seen *Life Magazine* photos of the Black Panthers with guns but assumed those guns were just stage props. Marsha glanced anxiously towards Mrs. Baker.

A square middle-class woman, Mrs. Baker was almost as old as Marsha's mother. People said Mrs. Baker was a communist who had fled to Canada during the McCarthy witch-hunts. She was a leader in the *Voice of Women*, all older women peaceniks. Mrs. Baker even looked like Marsha's mother, with short wavy dark hair, a pale flowered blouse, a navy blue sweater and dark framed glasses. She might be square, but Marsha hoped she would know what to say about the guns. Mrs. Baker calmly looked at the big Panther woman.

"We don't own any guns. And we don't know where to get guns," she said. "We can give you housing."

"You can stay at my house," said Marsha. She smiled up at the two women. "What are your names?" The women looked so powerful and beautiful. Marsha really wanted to take them home and introduce them to Ran. They would probably trust him since he was Japanese Canadian, sensei, not white. The Panthers had Asian *Yellow Power* allies.

The shorted thinner woman smiled. "My name is Rosie," she said.

"We don't tell our names," said the bigger woman. And Rosie shrank back. "And we don't stay with you, Whitey! Now give us your housing list," she said.

"We will give you addresses for your group," said Mrs. Baker.

"We don't take orders from Whitey," said the big woman. It was as if angry sparks were shooting off the edges of her Afro hair.

"Right on," said Marsha. "You can sit here next to me and pick the housing yourself."

"No, they can't see the lists," said Mrs. Baker. "It's confidential information."

"Oh, it'll be O.K.," said Marsha passing the whole pile of housing lists to the big woman.

"I'll just take them for a minute," the big woman said. She grabbed the lists and stomped out. Her partner, Rosie, looked surprised as she rushed out. Marsha was confused and didn't know whether to run after the two of them, or just wait for them to return with the housing lists. After a few minutes, it seemed like they weren't about to return. Marsha stepped into the hall and asked, "Does anyone know where they went?" No one knew.

"Do we have copies?" asked Marsha.

"No," replied Mrs. Baker. "Luckily the Vietnamese delegation was picked up at the airport, so we don't need to worry about them… Well… we better find some other housing quickly."

Mrs. Baker calmly reached under the table and pulled up her black patent leather purse, rummaging in it for her address book. She started phoning all her friends and sending the waiting delegates to their homes. Marsha phoned Kim and told her the problem.

"Kim we are really stuck; could you please take some delegates?"

Kim laughed. "That's too funny! The black women ran off with your lists. Don't even think of sending anyone to my place. What if my parents found out?"

Marsha didn't have time for persuasion. She called Ran.

"We are short of housing, so I need to send a big delegation from Los Angeles to our house. They've got sleeping bags, but can you find some pillows and cushions?"

"Sure. That's great. Send as many as you want," he said. "I'll come to the conference after I settle them in."

Marsha turned to the next woman in line. It was Jean.

"Jean I'm very sorry but a Black Panther woman ran away with our housing list and we are looking for more housing. Can you wait a bit?'

"That's cool. I understand. I wouldn't mess with that big woman. In Oregon, the Panthers don't want alliances with us. They won't even speak to us. I'll go talk with my delegates," said Jean, leaving the office.

"Why do they want guns, and why don't they trust us?" asked Marsha.

Mrs. Baker shrugged.

"Is it just because we are white, or gay or what? We aren't racist. Aren't we their allies?" asked Marsha.

"We need to find more housing," said Mrs. Baker. "And those lists were supposed to be confidential."

Ran called back saying they could fit lots more people on cushions on the floor. Marsha was thinking it would be lovely if Jean could stay with them. Mrs. Baker was finding more housing by going cover to cover through her little black phone book. After a while, Jean returned.

"I went to that Lutheran Church down the street. The minister or priest or whatever he is said our whole delegation can sleep on the floor at his church. They've got a carpet, washrooms, even showers and a kitchen," she said.

"I guess that Lutheran priest is a progressive," Mrs. Baker said. "And it's possible that Black Panther woman who took our lists was an FBI agent."

"Oh, no way," said Marsha. "The Panthers are so strong. They are involved demonstrating and organizing those breakfast programs. They know each other like sisters and brothers. They couldn't be FBI," said Marsha. "All this talk about infiltration and agent provocateurs. That's from spy books. It doesn't happen here in Vancouver."

Mrs. Baker looked at Marsha. "You'd better get going. The plenary session is getting started. I can finish up here."

"Thanks Mrs. Baker."

Only women were allowed past the guards into the plenary, women, Black Panther men, and Ran. The largest hall on campus was packed with excited students, adults, and newspaper cameramen talking and looking for chairs or spaces to sit on the floor. Ran was right up at the front with his Nikon. Marsha found some space against a sidewall squeezed next to some very fat lesbians from Los Angeles. They had lots of badges on their denim jackets.

The stage was flanked by two stern Black Panther women with guns. A tall thin North Vietnamese women stood to speak. There was silence. She was gaunt in a high neck black cotton shirt and pants, her face deeply scarred. She slowly shuffled to the microphone. Her interpreter, a small man also dressed in black, stayed close to her.

"I am Dinh Thi Huong, a housewife from my village in North Vietnam. I was not political. But my husband was killed, and there was just me and my daughter. She was only 13 when the soldiers came and took her. She was tortured."

Marsha looked away. She looked at Ran focusing his Nikon. She glanced at the big women next to her, wiping tears from their cheeks.

"Then they came for me. I was beaten and thrown in a filthy cell packed with naked men, women and children. I knew one of the women, a neighbour and her son Bihn. He was a sweet little four year old who loved flowers. Sometimes he used to bring me flowers. Every day someone in the cell died. One morning little Bihn was dead and his mother refused to give him up. They beat her senseless."

Mrs. Dinh Thi Huong's voice became even quieter. "They took me to the torture room for questioning. But I knew nothing. They put pins under my fingernails and electrodes on my earlobes, my nipples, my genitals. They forced water and lime into my stomach and then jumped on me. I had nothing to tell them. They hung me from my hands and beat me until I became paralyzed."

"They wanted me to admit that I was a member of the liberation struggle. But I was not involved. Finally, I was found not guilty and released. My friends were amazed that I had survived. The prison staff hoped that the example of my torture would scare my village. However we were angry. I decided to join the fight against the Americans and their puppets."

Marsha and the whole audience were silent. People around her were crying, angry. Marsha found Ran. "Let's go home."

"Yes…do you think her daughter survived?"

"I don't know."

"I got some great close-ups of her face."

"Ran it's not fair. Just because you are Japanese Canadian, you can go to all the sessions - black, white, or lesbian. And I worked so many hours for the conference but I'm not allowed in."

"You're right," said Ran.

"Anyway, Ran, you can't come with me to the party to-night. It's just for women.'

"That's OK. I've got to develop my photos."

Marsha was exhausted and tempted to stay home with Ran in their warm house but she really wanted to attend this new type of event, an All Women's Party.

Clutching the steering wheel of the blue Datsun she peered through the rainy windshield looking for the Morningstar Collective. It felt strange driving alone. She went to every social event with Ran. Friends joked that they were joined at the hip. Despite their closeness, Marsha had often felt lonely and empty until that first moment she kissed Kim's lips and lost herself in Kim's soft body.

"You just find my skin soft because I'm a woman," said Kim laughing.

Marsha knew it was more than just enjoying Kim's smooth body and welcoming breasts. Suddenly all of Marsha's body came alive. She kept touching and smelling herself in amazement. She felt like a new different person. More herself. If only Kim was coming to the party with her it would be so cool. However Kim would never come to an All Woman's Party.

The Datsun's windshield wipers were not terribly effective. Luckily Marsha was intimately familiar with the Kitsilano hippy neighbourhood because she worked in community mental health. Here was the drug house where the cops beat up her classmates, and there was the old apartment with the young mother suffering from post partum psychosis who mistook Marsha for a drug dealer, and there was the basement where the young hippie almost immolated himself, and there was that house where the landlady wouldn't rent to her and Ran because Ran wasn't white. And there was the Morningstar Collective, the house with the turret and peeling paint, just across the road from the beach.

She climbed the wet slippery steps of the old wooden house, wiped her boots on the doormat, opened the door and was hit by a barrage of loud music and smoke. She coughed and walked down the hallway to the bright lights of the kitchen. It was solidly packed with women all drinking, smoking, and talking. Could tiny Vietnam really defeat the USA? When was violence politically correct? What about the Black Panthers? Racism, Sexism, Women's Liberation, Lesbian Liberation? When is Personal Political? Is making love with a woman as effective as demonstrating? Marsha saw the world changing right before her eyes.

But her vision blurred. The smoke was too much for her allergies. Eyes burning, she retreated into the dimly lit front room. *All you need is love* blared from the stereo. She walked across the bare, gritty, wooden floor towards a pile of torn stained cushions scattered against the wall. A circle of six or seven women clung to each other in the center of the room swaying to the music of John Lennon. In the corner below the window, a large woman was lying on top of another woman. They were kissing and touching each other intimately. Marsha quickly looked away. How could they do that in public? A tall blond woman was leaning against the wall.

It was Jean, from Corvallis. Marsha smiled at her as she peeled off her wet raincoat and dropped it on the floor.

"Hi Jean. It's sure pouring outside. I'm Marsha from the registration office."

"Yes, I remember you. Does it always rain like this in Vancouver?"

"Yah, most of the winter you can't even see the mountains. But remember yesterday was sunny?"

"Right, yesterday. So much has happened since yesterday," said Jean.

"Have the Lesbian Caucus sessions been good?" asked Marsha.

"Well there's lots of dissent. I wonder if this's really the best time to try'n teach the Vietnamese women about Gay Lib. After all they're fighting for their lives and getting napalmed. Oh. The speaker at the plenary - do you think her daughter is still alive?"

"I don't know."

"Also, I'm really bi-sexual."

"Oh really? Me too! I live with my husband, and I'm lovers with a woman, Kim. But she's too paranoid to let anyone know."

It was the first time Marsha had told anyone about Kim or about being gay. She looked at Jean's blue eyes and thick brown eyebrows. Jean was quiet. Marsha felt that Jean was really listening to her, and she had to resist the impulse to reach up and stroke Jean's long, thick hair. Then Marsha started coughing. This always happened at parties. She would be having fun and then get a sore throat and runny nose.

"Sorry. I'm allergic to smoke," she said.

"Even pot?" Jean said.

"Yah. It's a drag."

"Too bad. Want to go outside and talk on the porch?"

"Sure let's go to the beach. It's just across the road."

Outside the air was clean and cold, the rain dwindling to drizzle and mist. The lights from downtown sparkled on the water. Jean spoke with an American drawl in a lovely low voice. She was swinging from a low cedar branch that stretched over the sand and rocks. A wet wind blew against their faces. They clambered over the logs, slippery splintery wood under their hands, gritty sand on their shoes, and the smell of kelp. They crouched out of the wind in the shelter of a towering cedar. Jean said she lived in a rambling old farmhouse outside of Corvallis. She was wearing a heavy, navy pea jacket. Marsha could smell the scent of wet wool and wanted to rub her face on that woolly sleeve.

"There are four in our commune, two women and two men. We are all lovers with each other, and we share everything: cooking, money, sex."

Marsha's heart was pounding louder than the waves. An ache ran through her hands and arms.

"You make schedules of who sleeps with who?"

"Yes."

Jean's voice had deep musical notes. The clouds parted briefly, and moonlight lit her face with silver light. Marsha felt a wave of energy. Time and her whole future seemed to stretch out far across the Pacific Ocean to Japan, to Asia, to endless possibilities. It was as if she had the strength to break all bonds of family and society and go anywhere and do anything. She thought if only she could hold this moment and stay at the beach with this woman forever...

Jean turned away. "I'm getting cold. Let's go back to the party."

"O.K."

They trudged back to the party. Almost as soon as they entered the house Jean's group was leaving.

"Jean, could I have your address?" Marsha asked.

"Sure! See you at the conference."

The next morning Marsha kept looking for Jean but only saw her once across a crowded hall. By the time she pushed through the crowd, she was gone.

Things started to change. One day a young RCMP officer arrived at the house to interrogate Marsha and Ran. Later the phone rang, and when Marsha picked it up, she heard a click, like the phone was bugged. It was Hank, the old man who arranged safe houses for draft dodgers.

"Hi Marsha have you any space at your house?"

"Sorry, you've got the wrong number." Marsha quickly hung up the phone.

"Ran," she said. "Mrs. Baker must've been right. I should've protected those fucking housing lists."

"Yes," said Ran.

"Do you think they'll catch Hank? asked Marsha.

"Hope not."

Someone had stuck a cartoon on the kitchen wall. It was a picture of a policeman beating up a young man. The young man was saying "But I'm an anti-communist." And the cartoon cop was saying, "I don't care what kind of communist you are."

One day Marsha came home to find Jeff, their housemate, cleaning two rifles on the kitchen table.

"Fuck Jeff! What if someone sees you?"

"It's cool. They aren't loaded. Besides didn't you hear about the bomb chemicals Barb found at the coffeehouse?" said Jeff.

"Yah but Barb told me she kicked those guys out before they blew up the SFU Shell Station," said Marsha.

Marsha thought the extremists kids were nuts, maybe, or was now actually the time for armed struggle? She began teaching Women's Self Defense courses. She was feeling stretched in her three way relationship with Ran and Kim. Kim came over to Marsha and Ran's house one morning and began tearing their posters and smashing their teacups. Ran was suspicious. Someone was always getting hurt.

Marsha still didn't really understand how the personal was political. She must do something to stop that war, change society, but what?"

"Ran let's move to a commune in the country."

"Sure, smoke dope, get hepatitis. I've lived in the country. Remember the Japanese relocation?"

Marsha wrote to Jean in Corvallis. There was no reply. A few years later when driving through Oregon she tried to phone Jean, but the number was out of service.

Faith

Jarren Gillaspie

Motivational speakers like to say that our inner world is reflected in our outer world. Well, that seemed the case in 1989. The Exxon Valdes crashing and spreading toxic sludge over our pristine coastlines in March mirrored the crash of my own toxic relationship, and as the tanks rolled through the streets to Tiananmen Square wiping out protestors en route, I'd packed up my objections and moved out of the West End to North Vancouver. By the time the Berlin Wall came down in November, I was coming into a newness of my own.

But let's begin with my Exxon Valdes, David. Physically he was an incredibly beautiful man. He modeled part-time while studying in an aesthetics program. We were both adult children of alcoholics. I was the eldest and over-responsible. David was the youngest and irresponsible. We broke up and made up five times in five years. I remember wondering what crisis he would present next as he walked out for the final time. At this point, I felt I would be okay spending the rest of my life without a partner. And with that out of the way came the almost instinctual urge to have a child. It was a need to give back, to mentor, to just guide another young being along life's road and to know that I was responsible for that. Through my work, I had a lot of contacts with social workers, and so I started trying to foster a child. Over the next few weeks, I received several profiles of troubled young teens.

Then the call came. It wasn't the social worker; it was my younger brother, Russell. We always had an unusual but caring relationship, the redneck and the fag.

"Ha ha you sucker! Mr. Perfect! Mom and Dad's golden boy! I thought there was more in your closet than you were telling us. Well bro, we all have to pay the piper some time. Looks like it's your time."

"What are you babbling about Russell. Are you high?"

"No. But I have a letter here that sounds pretty interesting. Yeah. From some seventeen-year old girl looking for her daddy. Says her Mom's name is Simone. Ring a bell Bro? Wasn't Simone that pretty little French girl you dated before you told us you were gay? You are gay aren't you? Did you and Simone actually do the nasty?"

"God Russell! There's no hope for you. One of us must be adopted. I dated Simone, yes. The rest is our business."

"Well not any more Bro. All of the Gillaspies got this letter."

"Is there a phone number on that letter?"

"Sure is. Want it? Are you thinking of changing teams, Bro?"

"Just give me the damn number."

I called right away. It rang several times before a woman answered. It had been seventeen years, but the voice hadn't changed. "Simone! It's Farren."

"You got a letter? I'm sorry. I told her not to try, that it wasn't fair to you, but she has her own ideas.

"Simone. She says I'm her dad."

"Well, you are, Farren. Remember when we decided to go our separate ways, and I came back to see you at the farm one last time? It was a special weekend, wasn't it?"

"I remember it feeling like goodbye, Simone."

"Well it was. But after I got back to Ottawa, guess what? I knew you and I wouldn't work, but I wanted a kid, and Diane said she'd help me. Knowing it was yours was special. I really wanted you to be the father of my first."

I sank deeper into my old leather Lazyboy as I listened, stunned.

"I did something very wrong though. Not only did I not tell you, but I told Faith that you hadn't wanted anything to do with us. I thought that would put a stop to her questions, but I was wrong. It just made her sad. I didn't really see it at first. Then just after her sixteenth birthday, her boyfriend committed suicide. I was worried, Farren. She was crying and asking what was wrong with her, so I told her the truth. I told her not to try to reach you because I didn't think it was fair, and I guess I knew I should have told you from the beginning. I was so foolish and independent then. I'm so sorry you had to find out this way."

"Simone I have to ask. Are you absolutely sure?"

"You'll know when you see her. She's a Gillaspie."

"Simone, a whole lot happened after that weekend. I forced myself to realize that I was actually gay. Well, at first I eased into it by convincing myself I was bisexual. I have been out as gay now for a long time."

"I'm not surprised. You weren't like most of your friends," she hesitated. "In a good way. Are you happy?"

"Actually not that happy right now. I've had a couple of really crappy relationships. The last was the worse. We broke up so many times I saw more of the back of his head than the front. But it's done. And now this. It all seems so surreal. If I fly back, can I meet her?"

"Of course!"

"It will take a couple of weeks to get covered at work. I'll call you as soon as I get a date."

I was still walking around in a daze the night the phone rang. When I answered, it was David. *What now?* I thought. *How can you better your last crisis?*

"I need to see you Farren."

"Sorry David. That's not a good idea."

"I have some news I need to share with you."

"David is your Mom okay?"

"She's fine. It's about us."

"David please, there is no us anymore. Just say what you have to say."

"Farren. I have AIDS. Not just the antibodies. I have it all." He started crying.

I have always been able to think quickly on my feet and respond intelligently. This time I sat down in a blur. What kind of joke was this? The Universe gives me a child I never knew I had, and now, it takes my life. I took a deep breath.

"David we went to the AIDS awareness seminars together. We agreed we would always have safe sex when we weren't together."

"Sorry Farren." He started sobbing and hung up.

That phone call was the last I ever heard from him. I heard from friends that, true to our former patterns, he accelerated his party agenda and passed away a year later in Toronto, where he'd moved to be near his brother.

Meanwhile, I raided all of my cupboards, throwing out anything that remotely resembled junk food, white sugar, jams, processed foods, the works. I fasted, changed my vitamin regime, and rejoined the gym. My mania was interrupted by a friend who pointed out the obvious, so I went and got tested, so that I would know where I stood with this virus.

A very supportive nurse at the clinic did the test for me. I tearfully told her my story about Faith. How I had wanted a child so badly. Someone I could nurture and love. Now, I would die on her like her boyfriend, or worse, she would have to look after me until I died.

When I returned for the results, she came around from her desk. She was smiling, but I thought, *this is bad.*

"You are negative," she said as she gave me a hug. "You seem really healthy, so I'm sure the antibodies would have shown up already, but we will have to test you again to be really sure."

The second test was negative as well.

The good news came just before I headed back to Ontario. I could have flown without being in the plane.

When I entered Simone's home, Faith was standing behind her. At seventeen, she could have been my sister's twin at that age. "Well Faith. It's been seventeen years and five thousand miles."

We hugged. This tall slender, vulnerable girl in my arms was actually part of me. Unbelievable. I choked and silently gave thanks.

Faith came to stay with me that summer. My gayness was of no consequence to her.

"I tried to have sex with my girlfriend once Dad. Sorry, but it was pretty gross."

Father and daughter went shopping. I think she must have worn heels when she first learned to walk. She was never out of them. To pacify me, she actually tried on a few skirts, but tight skinny jeans were her comfort zone. She was a teaser, much like myself. A couple of times when we got to the checkout, she would give a treacherous smile and in her sexiest voice say, "Thank-you Daddy. You are so good to me!" The cashier would grin, and I'd turn red. I would threaten that if she did that again I'd walk out. Of course she did, and of course I didn't.

She insisted on going to the clubs to see where I went dancing. "Heels were made for dancing, Dad."

"You can't drink, Faith."

"But I can dance, Dad."

She hardly left the dance floor. When drag queens weren't exclaiming over her long legs or her heels, handsome young men were hitting on her.

"I thought this was a gay bar Dad. Why are these guys hitting on me?"

"Guess it's a different time Faith. Young people don't seem to care about labels anymore."

"So some of them might be straight?"

"Yes. Or bi, or questioning."

She headed back to the dance floor. Not long after she came back towards me followed by yet another handsome young man.

"Jared. This is the man I have been looking for all of my life."

His well-defined chest sunk.

"My Dad."

Stonewalled

Christine Waymark

From the radio I hear the news of riots in New York, gay men and drag queens in a place called Stonewall. They are rioting because of a police raid. I grit my teeth as I bend to pick up the kids laundry for the day. Karen, thumb in mouth, is sleeping after her 6am feed. Four year old Stephen, already in the back garden, will be occupied enough with his trucks and the sand. Janet, soon to be three, and Kevin, five, have sheets of newsprint, crayons, and felt pens on the dining room table. They'll be okay together until I get the first load into the wringer washer.

All I can think is *"Why aren't women rioting?"*

My back and belly ache from the tubal ligation a few days before. Even with the diagnosis that another pregnancy could mean a wheelchair for the rest of my life, I've had to see four male doctors and get my husband's permission to get the surgery. Where are *my* rights? Who's protesting for me? It's *my* body and *my* life. I'm the one who carries and births the children. I'm twenty-nine years old, mature enough to raise a family, but apparently my husband owns my womb.

I grab the basket of clothes and put it on my right hip, where I often carry a child. Flicking on the light, I hold the basement door open with my bum and continue down the steep wooden stairs and through the unfinished playroom to the laundry area at the back of the house. I keep my ears tuned to the sounds upstairs, ready to run. I know I'll have to carry the wet laundry back upstairs to hang it on the line that runs from the back porch to the end of the garden.

My rage terrifies me, so I bury it. Childhood taught me that my job was to help Mum make life easier for my dad and my brothers. I married at twenty. It was the only legitimate way to leave home. I'm glad that my eldest is a boy. I won't, even unconsciously expect him to be a parent. He'll be encouraged to drive and go to university. He won't be told to use his intelligence to raise clever sons.

Later that night, I check each child on my way to bed. Coming to the bedside of my eldest, I think about how Kevin prefers to draw, read, and practice piano than play outside with other children. His brother is impossible to confine. What does that make Kevin? The news of Stonewall is fresh in my mind. Could Kevin be gay? Will he grow up to be a drag queen? What could make a man want to dress like a woman? What could make a man love another man? If I can see it in Kevin, is it from birth?

My brother's friend is a drag queen and Mum says it's because his mother let him dress up as a girl when he was little. She doesn't think her grandsons should have dolls or even stuffed animals. Mum tried to escape the poverty of a cotton mill town when she married Dad. When he couldn't get work in post war England, she engineered our immigration to Canada. Mum uses her intelligence to run community organizations as well as her family of five children. She manages all the family finances, but has never earned any money of her own.

****

The office has a very large desk with a couple of framed pictures and a large framed blotting pad in front of the big black leather chair. The bank manager is prompt. "Good afternoon, Mrs. Partridge," he says, hand outstretched. I reach and shake it, wondering why I am here. This is the third time I've renewed our mortgage.

"We have your application for the mortgage renewal and see that you are applying alone."

"Yes, my husband left in 1973, and the house is now legally mine."

"Would you have a brother or a father who would co-sign with you?"

I look at him, trying to get his meaning. "I've been making the payments, and the house is in my name."

"Mrs. Partridge, all banks in Canada have the same policy. A woman can't hold a mortgage or have any credit of any sort. Surely, you have a male relative who will sign for you?"

Where are my rights? I am raising the children alone and now I can't have a mortgage?

Why aren't women rioting?

****

This time, the office is a basement room in a United Church. I sit in the circle of four men and two women, all of us on metal folding chairs. This committee oversees me and other students who are candidates for ministry. I have been here several times and know the routine, so I'm quite relaxed.

"We hear you live with another woman, does that mean you are a lesbian?" asks the new chairperson.

Mind racing, I think of my options. He isn't supposed to ask me this question, but not to answer would be evasion. Denial isn't possible for me. I have more rights as a woman and now I take the next step.

"Yes," I reply.

About the 1980s and 1990s

Elise Chenier

Happy Pride!

By 1980, most large urban centres in Canada and the United States had some kind of defined lesbian and gay culture that consisted of a few gay male bars and bathhouses, a lesbian bar (although these rarely lasted very long), a bookstore, a locally produced newspaper or newsletter, a weekly show on co-op radio, a coming out support group, and increasingly, spiritual groups like the lesbian and gay Catholic group *Dignity*. Toronto, New York, and San Francisco were large enough to even support a lesbian and gay theatre company. And every year, more and more people poured into the downtown "gaybourhood" for the annual pride march. This was the infrastructure upon which today's massive urban queer communities were built.

Change and *challenge* continued to be the defining features of mainstream lesbian, gay, trans and queer life through to the end of the century. First, people of colour and trans people burst onto the scene with new organizations, both cultural and political, which created important spaces and facilitated the formation of community networks within the larger white lesbian and gay culture. Writers like Audre Lorde, Reinaldo Arenas and Alice Walker attracted enormous followings. Their work was taken up in women's studies programs across Canada and the US, but transsexual and transgender writers like Jan Morris would have a more challenging time gaining an institutional foothold. Another political voice to emerge was that of intersex people who challenged the medical normalization of bodies.

The larger these communities grew, and the more positive media coverage they generated, the easier it became for everyday people to resist pressure to fit into the pink and blue boxes laid out for them. Social support groups formed in every major urban centre to help folks make the difficult and often painful transition into a non-normative life.

Cruising was a major part of the urban queer scene, especially for gay men who celebrated an unfettered sexuality. When the AIDS crisis emerged in the late 1970s, it was an enormous blow on all levels. It affected people personally and politically, and it challenged the community socially, too. Given that so much of gay culture was built on the joyful celebration of sex and non-monogamy, how would gay male culture reinvent itself in light of the epidemic?

Fortunately, the infrastructure built up over the previous decade turned out to be a remarkably strong foundation upon which to mobilize a massive movement that would challenge governments, the medical system, and the pharmaceutical industry. New organizations like ACT UP emerged. Once again, lesbians joined gay men in their effort to bring about change, to save lives, and to help people die with dignity. Political tactics learned in the 60s and early 70s were re-fashioned. Art played a major role in the movement. Graphic artist Keith Harding's bold images, for example, became iconic. Plays like Angels in America and RENT, and movies like *Paris is Burning* and the big Hollywood breakthrough film *Philadelphia* brought difficult conversations about sex, gay men, and sexually transmitted diseases and infections into public discourse.

Women were engaged in a sustained debate about sex, too, although not with the deadly consequences the AIDS debates had. In the 1970s, more and more feminists saw pornography as both a representation of and an incitement to woman-hating. They also felt that sexual practices such as sado-masochism perpetuated power imbalances. Some even held that any kind of vaginal penetration was a form of rape, and opposed that, too. Not surprisingly, this pushed those whose sexual practices did not fit in to this model to form their own political, social, and artistic groups. Women's porn, leather, and BDSM cultures exploded on the cultural scene. They forced the lesbian community to have difficult political conversations about the nature of desire and the possibility of progressive, ethical sexual practice. Vancouver-based art collective Kiss'n'Tell explored these tensions in an enormously popular exhibit *Drawing the Line* in which a series of photographs depicting a lesbian couple – both collective members – engaged in increasingly graphic sexual acts. Viewers were encouraged to pick up a marker and draw a line where the images shifted from acceptable to unacceptable. They were also encouraged to comment, and they did. Art played a critical role in moving debates forward.

The rawness of these debates and the challenges that confronted lesbians and gays in the 1980s sharply contrasts with the decade of commercialization and neoliberalism that followed. In the early 1990s, corporate America and Canada discovered lesbians and gays as a valuable consumer market. Companies that sold liquor, banking products, and other goods extended their marketing plans to the white lesbian and gay (but not transgender or bi) communities by advertising products and services to them and by buying up space in annual Pride celebrations. Many saw this as a victory, but for others it signaled a troubling shift away from community grassroots organizing and a critique of heteronormativity to the celebration of consumer culture and the promotion of homonormativity. Tellingly, Pride Marches were re-named Pride Parades. Large corporate floats mostly overshadowed elements of political protest that dotted Pride events.

It was also in the 1990s that the word *queer* came into common usage. Discussions within groups like ACT UP led people to observe that their lives did not fit into the narrow category of *gay* or *lesbian*. Furthermore, their sexuality was fluid, not fixed. *Queer*, which had been a word of derision, was reclaimed and became, for some at least, a positive term. It also created a new binary: it replaced heterosexual/homosexual with normal/queer. It also breathed new life into the social critique of sex and gender norms that gay liberationists once championed.

By the 1990s, *lesbian and gay* became *LGBT*, an acronym that is now extended to include even more categories of difference such as *2* for two-spirited, *Q* for queer, and *Q* for questioning: *LGBTQQ2*. Such forms of recognition are helpful, but the reality is that people of colour, trans folk, bisexuals and indigenous queers are rarely at the centre of discussions or organizing unless they are doing it from within organizations and groups of their own. Similar tensions exist for the poor and working class, whose perspectives and points of view are not generally represented.

In 1983 the Canadian band Parachute Club released the song *Rise Up* to critical acclaim and widespread fame. The song implores listeners to "rise and show your power:"

We want lovin'
We want laughter again
We want heartbeat
We want madness to end
We want dancing
We wanna run in the streets
We want freedom to live in this peace
We want power
We want to make it ok
Want to be singin' at the end of the day
Children to breathe a new life
We want freedom to love who we please

By the end of the 1990s, it looked as if the freedom to love who we pleased had largely been won. But some also worried about what had been lost, and others felt still to be very, very far from the finish line.

Gay Pride

Drawn by Maggie Shore based on a photograph by Robin Rennie

Fairy

Robin Rennie

We found a perfect spot in the shade where we arranged ourselves along the curb. We were Grannie and Gramma, our excited four year old granddaughter, and her two cool teenage brothers. The parade passed before us, dykes on bikes, floats advertising gay bars and straight businesses. There were banners shouting *PFLAG! The Centre! Rainbow Refugees!* There were variously wheeled cycles and roving clowns. There was lots of interaction between parade participants and watchers. I had stood up to watch, just into the road, so people behind could see above me, as if I was actually tall.

A very slight, fair young man, one could say looking quite like a fairy, clad only in sky blue Capri tights, and clearly nothing else, came right up to me, face to face. He captured my eyes, then lowered his head in a way that my head and eyes followed his. He began to roll down his tights. I found myself transfixed, and could not tear my eyes away. He rolled them slowly, right down past his fair, whispy, and quite sparse pubic hair, and then even more slowly, all the way to the full Monty. After a moment, he once more looked me in the eye with both triumph and mischief, having *had* me. And then he tripped away gaily on into the middle of the parade and disappeared.

I was bamboozled. I had been hypnotized! A lesbian grandmother had been made to gaze at a man's genitals in front of her grandchildren at the Gay Pride Parade. It is an experience forever burned in my memory, and whenever it comes to mind, my brow furrows. How did he get me to do that?

Old Style Beer at B.J.s

Sandra Mudd

Carol parks her old yellow Volkswagen on Hamilton Street. I watch as she gets out of the car, dressed in her androgynous way in shades of grey with her big leather purse over her shoulder. Her long brown hair is as neat as the rest of her. This must be how she passes for straight at the office. As we walk down the hill past Victory Square, she points out the green dome of the Sun Tower, which for a short time, was the tallest building in Canada. We cross West Pender and turn into B.J.'s.

I notice the sign for a steam bath next door. What am I getting myself into? I follow her through the smoky darkness and over to the bar on the right. "What are you drinking?" Carol asks.

I glance at the bottles behind the bar. "Old Style." It's what everyone orders when we go for drinks after work.

We find a table with a good view of the dark stage right in the middle of the almost-empty room. There are mostly women – masculine, heavy-set women in jeans and plaid shirts. I really don't want to be there, but Carol thought I should meet some other lesbians. If I met someone I could date, that would let her off the hook. But I don't want to meet anyone else. If she doesn't feel the same way, why did she go to bed with me? Why did she wait till after we became lovers to tell me about her partner?

I look again to see if there is anyone here I could even want to talk to. As Carol excuses herself and heads slowly across the dance floor towards the bathroom, I feel the shock of the demands she'd made to allow me to even see her: no commitments, and any sign of drama and she'd be gone.

Left alone and scared, I study the garish red, yellow and green beer label as if my life depends on remembering every detail. That doesn't take very long. Next I experiment with peeling off the corners. The square label becomes round. Where is Carol? She can't still be in the bathroom. Then I see her talking to a woman across the room. I have the crazy thought that maybe she is trying to set me up with that person, but no, it looks like they are old friends.

I return to my beer. I feel the damp label under my fingernails and clean more off the bottle. Pretty soon it is half gone. Then Carol joins me again and lights up a cigarette. She laughs at the neat pile of wet paper in front of me.

"Have you checked out the action yet? There are some really interesting women here."

I mumble something noncommittal. It feels safe to look around now. I notice some women laughing and talking together at a table next to the wall. One of the group looks a bit like me - over-dressed for the occasion, eyes all around the room. As I watch the group, I see how protective they are of her. There is always someone with her even when the rest of the group gets up to socialize or go to the bar. I feel very vulnerable.

Then the stage lights up and the emcee introduces the first act - a man dressed up better than any woman I know. He wears a glittery, dark blue, tight-fitting dress that emphasizes breasts and long lean legs. The blond wig is perfect on top of the beautifully made up face. He sings *Over the Rainbow* and everyone applauds the choice. The distraction is comforting but I feel distant. Do all lesbians like listening to men in drag sing Judy Garland songs? Is that what being a lesbian requires? Does that make me *a Friend of Dorothy*?

I haven't even seen *The Wizard of Oz*.

The bar is filling up with men now. They are well dressed and attractive, and that makes me feel more comfortable. Boy, am I confused! I like the men better than the women. What am I doing here? The next act is a Joan Rivers impersonator whose original jokes are so funny that I relax as I laugh. Maybe I am being way too serious. Intense is the way Carol describes me - whatever that means.

The set is over. Carol asks "Are you ready to go?" In seconds I am up and leading the way to the exit, feeling happy to be going. I notice the music playing is new to me: "I will survive." Me too, I think. Now I feel brave enough to look people in the face, safe in the knowledge that there is no time to talk. Glad to be alone again with the woman I love who is nothing like the other women in the bar.

I did it!

I went to a gay bar. Now I don't need to go back.

Letters

Bridget Coll

Co. Donegal, Ireland
May 1951

My dear daughter Bridget,

We are all well here and I hope this will find you the same.

Yesterday I saw the postman coming over the lane on his bicycle. He walks in with the letter in his hand and says to me here is your latest from Bridget.

I am glad to hear that you are getting enough to eat. I was a bit worried because I hear stories that the convent can be strict. You say they have you looking after the hens. Well they could have nobody better. I'm sure they don't know much about hens in England.

Dadda is fine. He set the new potatoes. Mary is thinking of going to Australia. Margaret is the same as ever. She is going to Glasgow to do nursing. Tessie, Sarah Anne, Donald and Una are still at school. Nellie is the same as ever. We still send down her dinner. Uncle Neddy came over the other day and had his cup of tea then off he went.

The light keepers come up every day. We give them milk and eggs. Gertrude is going to join the nuns. We pray for you every night when we say the rosary.

I know that the Superior reads all your letters, but I am not going to change the way I write to you. We all miss you. A lot of the neighbours are asking about you.

That's all the news I have. I'll be looking forward to hearing from you next month.

With love and God bless you
From Mamma

My legs felt like jelly as I climbed the stairs to the Superior's office. I knocked softly on her door and waited for her gruff response. I knelt on the floor beside her desk as she spoke.

"Sister. I want to remind you that you are still a Novice and not a member of our congregation yet. Whoever puts his hand to the plough and looks back is not fit for the kingdom of heaven."

I thought I was to be sent home.

"I am not satisfied that you are following our rules when you write to your parents. You are to address them respectfully. What could be nicer than *Dear Mother and Father*?"

I kept silent. What was I to do? Never had I called my parents anything but Dadda and Mama. The next letter-writing Sunday came and I wrote my letter and signed it as I always did.

I waited for the reprimand.

It never came.

Dear Sister Gerard,

I am writing because of the death of your parents.

It must be a consolation for you to have seen them celebrate their golden anniversary. They are happy in heaven now and you must be happy about that too. You should be grateful that you will not have to be concerned anymore about their failing health. Now they will be looking down on you from heaven.

You will feel better when you get back to work in the parish.

We remember you and them in our prayers.

With prayerful sympathy,

Sister Mary Francis

When I got back to the convent after my parents' funeral, I said to Chris "I got letters from all the other Sisters, but none from you. Why have you not written?"

She said: "I didn't know what to say." Then she said, "How do you feel?"

That was the first time since my parents' deaths that anyone asked me how I felt. I knew then that I loved Chris and that she was the person I wanted to spend my life with.

Staffordshire, England
July 10th, 1977

Dear Sisters,

I am writing to remind you of the Birthday of our Congregation on the 8th of September. As you know, this is a very important occasion in our Congregation. It behooves us to celebrate in a fitting manner to honour the spirit of our Mother Foundress whose birthplace was in Rochdale, Lancashire. I would like to know how you are going to celebrate an occasion that will unite us all in whatever part of the world we may be serving, to better the lives of the people with whom we work.

Here in the Motherhouse, we are going to celebrate at a garden party in Rochdale. The Mayoress has kindly offered to pick us up in her limousine. It will be fitting for us to celebrate in the birthplace of our Mother Foundress.

I will be coming to visit you soon. My assistant will write to you in the next two weeks to let you know the date of our arrival.

Sincerely in Christ,

Mary Alice FMSJ

Chris and I knew how we were going to celebrate.

We arrived on the main street in the city with our signs and placards that read: Bread – Work- Justice and Liberty and then we marched until we heard the sirens.

As someone shouted "the water cannons are coming!" we linked arms. Shortly after the cannon doused us, a tear gas canister exploded at Chris's feet and we sought refuge in an open door. Generally the storeowners close their doors to protect themselves, but one kind storeowner opened his door and we all squeezed in and sat on the floor sucking the lemons we'd brought as an antidote. Chris and I held on to each other so that we would not get separated as we coughed and gasped.

When the military had left and the crowd dispersed, we made our way to the bus that would take us back to our little home in the shantytown. The bus was crowded and we made our way to the back and held on to the ceiling straps. There were women laden with bags and bundles of vegetables, and some children in uniforms were on their way afternoon classes. Every few stops, young men got on the bus with guitars, sang a song, passed around a hat, murmured a quick thanks and got off.

Men occupied the rest of the seats on the bus. I saw one of them look at us and whisper to the man beside him: "Gringas Comunistas." A stream of water ran from our jeans down to the front of the bus.

Chabuca, our cockapoo, jumped at our legs as we unlocked the little wooden gate. Once inside we spoke in English. We could see the house next door through the wooden walls.

"What do you think about the way we celebrated our Congregation's Birthday?" I asked Chris.

Chris replied, "They wouldn't be impressed."

"Why do you think she is coming"? I asked.

She answered: " Who knows what they have up their sleeve, but I think they will separate us. Since we are the only two members of the Congregation left in Chile, they will probably give us another assignment."

I thought out loud, "Maybe when they come we could tell them we want to leave the Congregation."

"That's a good idea, We'll tell them that we want a year of exclaustration. That way they'll be financially responsible for us."

"I knew that you'd come up with something."

"We'll have to write that letter to Cardinal Ratzinger for a dispensation from our vows," Chris replied: "I think we have to go through the Congregation. The Superior informs the Congregation of Religious in Rome, then the form letter comes to us. I think that's the way it works."

The 30th of December in the year 1988

Prostrate at the feet of your Holiness,

I am requesting a dispensation from my vows taken in the Congregation

of Saint Francis. My reason for requesting this dispensation is:

_____

Do you have more than one reason for leaving the Congregation?

If so state them in the space below:

The Best of Leonard Cohen

Gwyneth Bowen

Take This Longing

"Come over to my place for lunch?"

She's Swedish. A little younger than me at twenty-four but much more self-assured, she is gamine, coltish, with a blonde pixie cut and John Lennon glasses. I adore her. However, our only connection outside the world of my increasingly steamy fantasies is that we are colleagues in the same government social work office - and not even on the same team. No way to know whether our co-worker Eddie, who's an occasional bed buddy of mine (and probably of Eva's too), has told Eva that I am crazy about her, but from the way she's looked at me sideways a few times lately, I strongly suspect he has. Have they laughed about my infatuation?

"Uh, now? Um, that sounds good..." I try to sound cool while mentally aborting whatever my agenda was for the rest of the work day. We drive through a stifling London July in her hand-painted purple VW beetle to her top floor flat a few blocks away in Balham. As Eva makes ham sandwiches and pours two beers, she oh-so-casually mentions that the flat roof outside her bedroom window is perfect for sunbathing.

Susanne

Eva was a golden version of Fawn, whose naked body, ten years earlier, was the first in my life to move me to desire. She was fourteen, I fifteen, when we shared a girls' boarding school dormitory room with three others of varying ages. Nakedness was casual, accepted. Fawn had the colouring and eyes of a daughter of Cleopatra, and as we all undressed to put on our sadly unappreciated baby doll pj's, unwilling and unready for our institutional single beds as the windows still showed delicious summer evening daylight, I had to be careful to let my glance barely sweep her body and not stop to nuzzle her tender brown crannies and chocolate nipples. And yet, as I lay wide awake and wide open in my bed six feet from Fawn's, my hands on my breasts, I conjured in vivid sensual detail a faceless boy lying over me, penis stiff and aimed but never entering. The whole middle of me was a sucking, aching, urgent black hole... how did I never think to touch *down there*? I could say that fear of others hearing would keep me from it, but nor did I ever think of it in my room alone at home. Such wasted years! My dreams at fifteen sometimes treated me to an overnight sex change... evidently my unconscious could deal with me being a boy making love to a girl, if not the idea of two girls together, and I would wake aroused, confused, fascinated with the games my mind was playing with my hormones.

So Long, Marianne

A week or three before Eva's offer of lunch, I'd had another invitation from a less exciting source, though it led to a memorable evening. Patty, another colleague, had tickets for a Leonard Cohen concert. Did I want to go with her? *Did I want to go?* I would have gone with Margaret Thatcher if necessary... I was sheepish knowing how little I cared about Patty as a companion, but not ethical enough to be ashamed or to turn the chance down. It wasn't till after the concert in the smallish, dark, weed-infused hall with its muddy acoustics, that I realised what shy, plain Patty's hopes had been for my companionship. I saw clearly the chain of attraction... Patty, turned towards me, myself turned away, reaching out to Eva. Nothing was said; no-one was touched, but I was kind and a little distant with Patty after the concert, and she did not approach me again.

Bird on the Wire

January 1977. I have a one-way ticket for the 17th, my 28th birthday, to Vancouver, BC. I have promised my Canadian boyfriend Karl that I will live with him and decide about getting married before too long. I really love Karl, but I'm jittery about giving up my life in England, the closeness to my family, my own flat, my job... mostly I've been closing my mind and heart to all the losses, but there's one loose end, a nagging question, that seems symbolic of something, or like a corner that needs some light shone into it. I haven't seen Eva for months, since she left the office. I stop pacing around the flat and pick up the phone. It takes me a while to untangle the cord, but eventually I dial. I tell Eva I'm leaving for Canada. I ask her to join me for a drink. The receiver is slippery in my hand...

She says, "Ah." She knows what I'm asking. There's a noticeable pause. She says, "You remember Tom? The psychiatrist? We're engaged... I'm pretty busy planning the wedding..." I never did like Tom. I make small talk for a few minutes and wish her well before hanging up. Maybe I'll never have the answer to that question.

I'm Your Man

I am married to Karl for 22 years, good years, before that question becomes so hugely urgent that I need to leave him to find the answer.

Hey, That's No Way to Say Goodbye

My second Leonard Cohen concert is the best concert - bar none - I've ever been to in my 60 years. Thirty thousand people of all ages and demographics filling the BC place stadium in Vancouver for this stop on Cohen's 2009 world tour are ecstatic along with us, and the energy is electric. I'm with my partner of ten years, and, by a neat fluke, it's her birthday: she's sixty-one. Leonard Cohen is by now the consummate performer; I am hanging on every word. And as Leonard sings, "tonight will be fine... for a while," I don't know that Val is also in the audience, as yet unknown to me, and unimagined.

Margaret, if you're reading this, I don't want to write about our time together except to say that, as you and I relived in the divorce coach's office only yesterday, we came together in great passion, love, and hope, and determination to build a life together. There was so much about our relationship that was very, very fine.

Sisters of Mercy

In Eva's sunny living room, back in the sunny seventies, with the world still full of eager questions and hopes, I recognise the come-on in Eva's suggestion about sunbathing. Dr. Hook is singing "I'm gonna love you a little bit more." My throat is clogged with all my midnight fantasies about Eva's live, athletic body and the glances she's been giving me as she bends over the desk in the intake room, her tank top gaping low. I'm relatively comfortable with my own nakedness after all those years at boarding school, and she is clearly ok that way too, because, oh god, she's peeling off her jeans. I mentally review my route to nakedness... is that the way this is going? I can't hear my older self desperately urging from the future, "GO! For god's sake strip! Don't turn away now! Nnooooo...." But the moment has passed.

I have remembered that this morning I put on my very oldest, holiest, laundromat-greyest once-pink Marks and Spencer's underwear. I kick off my huaraches, shrug off my batik shirt, and, hitching up my jeans, step out onto Eva's private patch of rooftop to focus very hard on the ham sandwich she has made me.

Then we go back to the office.

There Ain't No Cure for Love

The present. The present is a gift, we are cheesily, breezily reminded, and it is. It's a Vancouver winter. My mum just died. We have two friends who are having major surgery; we have a friend who made it through a recent heart attack; we have three friends with cognitive decline, and a friend who is dying. We have lots of friends who are fine. My new, dear partner Val has MS. That's actually how we discovered that our attraction to each other was mutual - when she told me about her diagnosis. We went from an exciting new friendship to being sixty-odd going on seventeen, as we fell in love. We don't care about the age of our underwear... each other's health and the hope of a good night's sleep is more of a concern, and even that is forgotten utterly as we hold each other tenderly and, more often than I could have believed possible, with deep and joyful passion. We want this to be forever and dream sometimes about wedding plans. Most days, I'm pretty much convinced, almost all the time in fact, that the plan I grew up with - of one marriage for life - is not the only right way. What I do know is that the path that's led me, with only a few stumbles, here to this place has been the right one for me.

The Flute Player

Chris Mann

We had no idea why this blond hulk of a kid in an oversized navy ski jacket had to lurk in our front hall every Wednesday after supper till Dad was ready. He stood there making heavy breathing sounds, crinkling his noisy coat, and letting his boots drip water all over the floor.

What a loser.

"Kids, you be nice to Doug. Your dad is driving him to Scouts," Mom cautioned.

Yeah. Yeah. Yeah. There goes the Scout Master looking out for the underdog again. Yeah, about as interesting as the current Great Canadian Flag Debate.

Underdog indeed. I'd pulverized that underdog after he knocked over a broom in the hallway at school, and it wacked Carol across the face.

"You lay offa my sister, you hear?" I'd yelled.

It was the sixties, and though I wasn't normally a scrapper, I'd relished jumping on this kid's chest and head like he was my personal trampoline. He didn't fight back.

By the time Expo 67 came to Montreal, I'd joined the high school band. When I told Mr. Cole, the Band teacher I wanted to play the saxophone, he laughed. "An 80 pound *girl* playing the saxophone? What a joke!" Mr. Cole spat. "Play the flute like all the other little girls." Mr. Cole made us wear red uniforms with gold trim and we had to stand up when he entered a room. One time, a trombone player didn't stand up, and Mr. Cole tore through the crowds, knocking down chairs and music stands to grab the boy by the shirt. "I am in command here. Get off your butt. I mean it!" he yelled, pulling him up. When Doug turned up to join the band with a flute under his arm, I kept looking at Mr. Cole, but he just let him be. The only boy in the whole flute section. We all shook our heads.

The first day Doug asked me to have lunch with him, I wondered why. Didn't he remember our fight? On our fifth lunch together, Doug finally leaned close to me, a tall blonde Adonis with eyes deeper than the Mediterranean. He told me about his father. "He hates me, Chris. I never want to go home," he confided. "He yells at me, kicks me. He throws me out of the house." I could feel my heart speed up. "He wants me to be like my brother and play football. He hates it that I play the flute. He calls me a wimp. He told me I am not his son." Doug leaned his arm on the cafeteria table, avoided the ketchup glob, and slid his right sleeve up to his elbow to reveal a fist sized purple bruise. "I have more of these," he said. "I've been locked up in the basement while the rest of the family eats dinner. I've been chained to a post in the back yard. No one knows." There were no Social Services in those days. About the best you could do was have a nice guy like my dad around for Scout nights.

One evening when Doug and I were walking home from a Band concert with the horn section from "Pomp and Circumstance" still ringing in our ears, he told me he didn't understand how men and women had sex together. "How do they do it?" he asked. I was surprised he didn't know this yet. So, I grabbed his hand and ran to the shadows behind the bleachers on the field. I lay flat on my back on the grass with my legs spread open, and said, "Doug, you can pretend to lie on top of me, and you'll see how the parts are supposed to fit." In a few seconds, we were on our way again, but Doug was quiet all the way home. He just seemed perplexed.

High school came to an end. College started, and kids moved out. I had started working in a small town along the riverside and Doug was going to a local college in the same area. He found a small apartment on the second floor of an old four-story building on a street lined with maples, and four of us moved in for a year. The wooden floor creaked, the toilet ran, and the shower was mouldy. It didn't matter. We bought one copy of the *Joy of Cooking*, and moved through the book like researchers determined to master a new experiment each night. Doug discovered a recipe for Welsh rarebit and it became one of our favourites. The only time we had dessert was when we made cake for someone's birthday. Soon we invented half birthdays in order to have more cake.

In November that year, Doug came home beaming. He had found Jesus. "When did this start?" I asked.

He confided in me that he thought he might be gay, and since he didn't know what to do or who to talk to, he'd gone to a church two blocks away. "They are doing special programs there to help me," he said, turning his head to look out of the window at the bare trees.

"What do you mean – special programs?" I asked.

"You know, exorcism kind of things," he said. "A group of people pray for the Devil to leave me. They light candles and chant and put their hands on my head and shoulders while I kneel on the ground. I think it's working! I have accepted Jesus as my saviour, so I'm not gay. I'm so happy!"

By the time Prime Minister Trudeau married Margaret Sinclair, won another election, and welcomed defector Mikhail Baryshnikov, Doug was living downtown on his own. The first thing I noticed when I visited was the biggest jar of Vaseline I had ever seen sitting out on the kitchen table. I asked what it was for. "Have you heard of the Montreal Meat Market, Chris?" Doug asked. "It's where gay men go to have sex. I get picked up several times a night, and I need a lot of lube."

"What happened to Jesus?" I asked him.

"Jesus is in the toilet, along with all of us," he laughed.

Ten years later, I opened my mailbox one day to find a slim envelope with Doug's handwriting on it. By this time I had partnered with a woman, one of the roommates in our old shared apartment. We read the letter together.

> *Dear Chris – I have moved to Ottawa and have fallen in love. Tony is a renowned Chamber Orchestra conductor, and I have found peace with myself and with my faith at last. I'm working as a youth leader in Tony's church, and I'm a classroom assistant in a really nice school. I play my flute all the time.*
>
> *I want you both to come to meet Tony and see our wonderful home.*
>
> *love,*
> *Doug.*

Two years after we visited, Tony was dead.

Doug sold the house to pay for his AIDS medication and rented an apartment where a group of homophobic guys tormented him from their basement suite. Knowing that Doug's bed was in the living room, they hung a huge punching bag in the ceiling and whaled away on it for hours at a time. Thud. Thud. Thud. The whole floor vibrated.

"When did you know you were gay, Doug?" I asked that June.

"Well someone figured it out for me, when I was very young," he replied. "I was taken in a Chevy Nova after school every day for at least four days a week, during every year of high school and had my gayness pounded into me."

"Who did this, Doug?"

"Mr. Cole. The Band teacher."

In July, I was standing with the phone pressed to so close to my ear it left an indentation on my head. Doug's voice was a thin filament. "Chris, I need you to know that I'm ready to be with God. Tony has been gone for three months, and it's time."

"Doug, hang on! You still have lots to live for! I'm not ready for you to go!" I cried.

"I know, Chris, but I'm ready. All the arrangements are made. Look, I've sent you something. You should get it in a few days. Use it and remember me. I will always love you."

It was our last phone call. Doug died later that night. His father did not attend the funeral.

And a brown wrapped box did indeed arrive a few days later.

It was Doug's flute.

It's Because

Janie Cawley

My birthday celebration – dinner at my parents – epitomized my year. It isn't as though I was counting on a lot of fun. My first lesbian lover had moved out and acquired a new lover. This was *upsetting*, but being politically correct I found it *theoretically understandable*. And, of course, I never expect my kids to remember important dates outside of their own birthdays and when summer vacation began. But still, hope springs eternal. After all, the day was not without redeeming moments. The Fire Department did not have to be called to extract my younger daughter after she had launched herself down the book return shoot at the University. And, I did wind up my Wen-do class by breaking my board in three pieces with one fell swoop. Two pieces, I was given to understand, would have been sufficient.

In spite of these minor victories over the daily slog, I did not have a good feeling about the pending expedition into the parental domain.

On the way to dinner, my car got a flat tire. As a relatively new feminist, I had been working very hard to impress on my daughters that women could do anything men could do. I seized the opportunity presented by the flat tire as a teaching moment. Besides, I no longer had BCAA. "Well," I said. "We seem to have a flat tire. I guess we'll just have to change it ourselves."

My daughters were not impressed. Jean, thirteen and going through puberty, was already seriously disgruntled with the idea of spending time with the family. Her idea of an ideal evening was locking herself in her room and watching all of the soap operas she had recorded. Samantha, eight, was not keen on getting dressed up, which was a requirement for dinner at my parents. It had not been a cheerful car ride up to this point. However, when I changed the tire without a hitch, both girls looked moderately impressed. Unfortunately, the time it took to change the tire made us late for dinner.

Being late for dinner at my parents' place could and did have disastrous consequences. My father was a diabetic. When his blood sugar got out of balance, which it did when he didn't eat on time, he got grouchy. Very grouchy. "Where the hell have you been? Don't you know I have to eat my meals at regular times? Don't you ever think of anyone but yourself?" His greeting set the tone for the evening.

We settled quickly at the dinner table. Dad glanced at Jean. "Don't push your food on your fork with your thumb." He was probably excluding the use of all other digits as well.

Jean responded in a typically thirteen-year-old manner. "If I can't eat the way I want, I won't eat at all."

"Well, if you're not going to eat the way any civilized human being would eat, leave the table!"

"Nobody ever leaves me alone! Everybody is always picking on me! What about Sam? She isn't even using a fork!"

After this speech, Jean downed her utensil and made a beeline for the bathroom, slamming the door as only an indignant teenager can. Samantha, having had the spotlight turned on her, quickly got rid of the culinary evidence by wiping her hands on the crushed velvet chair upholstery. I looked at my mother to see if she had caught this violation of good manners.

My glance down the table at my mother confirmed that she had not missed anything on the manners front. Her jaw was clenched. She turned to me. "You know this wouldn't be happening if you weren't a lesbian."

"Wow, Mom," I said, "you shouldn't have kept this medical and sociological breakthrough to yourself for so long. I mean, if I weren't a lesbian, Dad wouldn't have diabetes, we wouldn't have been late for dinner, Jean wouldn't be going through puberty, and Samantha would have discovered the use of napkins, if not forks."

My mother glared. "You know very well what I mean."

Well, yes, I did. I'm clever that way. She meant she didn't like me being a lesbian. I excused myself from the table and went down the hall to the bathroom to try to talk with Jean through the closed door.

"Jean. Please let me in. We need to talk."

"No! Go away and leave me alone."

"Jean. Open the door."

"No. Can't a person get any privacy? Leave me alone."

"Jean. Be reasonable. It's my birthday. Open the door."

After several minutes we were all finally calmed down and back around the table just in time to do battle over who would light the candles on the birthday cake.

"Let me! Sam did it last time."

"I did not!"

"You did so!" said Jean. "Not only did you light the candles, you also set fire to the paper tablecloth and then put it out with the juice."

"Well, that didn't count. Mom, you're just letting Jean do it because she'll sulk and slam doors if she doesn't get her way."

"I'll light the bloody candles," my father yelled. "Can't you do something about these two?"

"No," I replied. "It's because I'm a lesbian."

Jean and Samantha sulked, my father glowered, my mother sighed and looked at the ceiling. I started to sing, "Happy Birthday to me..." Four reluctant voices joined in. We cut the cake and finished eating in silence. Then I said we really had to go because the kids had to get up early for school. No one protested. We got to the car.

"It's my turn in the front."

"It is not. You were in the front on the way here."

"Yeah, but you had two turns in a row before that so I get two turns."

"Oh my god", I thought. "Why am I fighting for custody of these two?"

Oh yeah. It's because I'm a lesbian.

Yukon Christmas

Harris Taylor

It's minus 40 degrees outside and the smoke from my wood stove is rising like a black poker in the blue, blue Yukon sky. People would be out skiing on a beautiful day like today, but my Christmas present to myself is a guest from Toronto.

She was impressed by my Mazda truck when I picked her up at the airport. She was struck by the splendour of the hoarfrost that coated every tree and rooftop with silver glitter. She was, I think, a bit turned on by the way I could steer with one hand and shift gears with the other while looking out for moose that might cross the winding road to my place.

When I removed my padlock, she was embraced by the scents of wood smoke and roast beef. A bold Shiraz, some smoked salmon, and we were ready to dine. We were hungry. Dinner was languorous. I knew from experience how weary she would be from the Toronto-to-Whitehorse-in-a-day journey. So, I invited her to lie down on my bed and rest while I warmed the wild cranberry crumble in the oven. Naturally, after a long day of cooking, driving and being on-the-lookout for moose, I was kind of whooped myself. So, I lay down beside her. Desert was burned beyond breakfast. Thus we remained, a pretzel of passion, horizontally entwined for six days.

On the seventh day, I heard the squeak, squeak, squeak of Sorrel boots on snow.

Knock, knock, knock. Shit!

Did I deadbolt the door behind us? Did the truck in my driveway insinuate that I was home with the kettle on? Who could guess what treats I might have cooked up in the last six days?

I answered the door in bare feet and bathrobe.

To my red-faced friend, I said, "No, no, not to worry. While most folks might not know it, I always walk around buck-naked day or night in my log cabin in the bush. It's always best to call in advance of a visit. And if I happen to be in the outhouse when you call, I do have an answering machine. So, I always, eventually, get the message."

Two weeks of bliss. The cross-country skis, which she had brought at my request simply gathered wood smoke dust.

Notes on Loving Your Neighbor

Harris Taylor

That winter was cold and lean. Our cabin was rough, but the quiet space was a refuge from my stressful job as a TV producer. Home was a wood fire and a hot meal that renewed my psyche after a long day. I was the only woman in the shop, an *out* lesbian who challenged colleagues about sexism, racism, and homophobia.

Everyone in Yukon was talking about the murder. Krystal Senyk, a 29-year-old employee of the Federal Government, had been shot dead at her home. Guns were missing from the Taggish Road home of her neighbor and suspected killer, Ron Bax. Bax was a blond, thirty year old hunter, taxidermist and sculptor, a crack-shot and well known for his survival skills in the bush. He had allegedly boasted his intentions to the other men drinking at the Caribou Hotel in Carcross. "I'm going to clean up this Territory, kill those man-hating lesbians. Cops won't ever find me."

Men in the bar had cheered him on. His stated intention to kill lesbians gave voice to widespread homophobia. The suspicion that he killed a woman who he believed was a lesbian made him a hero in the minds of some Yukoners. One of the guys at work hung a framed picture of Bax over his desk.

Krystal Senyk had been the female arm-wrestling champion of Yukon. She had lived alone in a cabin on Taggish Road. She'd been friends with Lynn Bax since they were children, and now they were neighbors. She knew that Lynn was being abused by her husband, Ron, and she helped her friend escape to the Whitehorse Transition Home for women fleeing domestic violence. I knew that because I also worked at the Transition

Home Friday and Saturday nightshifts. Senyk loved to live an independent life. That's why my lover and I lived 30 miles out of town.

One week after the murder, we heard the slow squeak of tires on snow in our isolated driveway. Heavy boots on the wooden porch. A knock at the door. We weren't expecting anyone at 8:00 pm. "My truck broke down," he said. "Been out cutting wood all day. Can I use your phone to call my wife?"

We were nervous but let him in.

"Hi honey, I'm stuck out by Takini Hot Springs. Don't know when I'll get home but didn't want you to worry. Taxi won't drive out this far. Guess I'll have to hitch. Tell the kids Daddy will see them in the morning. Be home as soon as I can."

"Well thanks," he said. "At least my family won't have to worry, and I'm warming up a bit now. Sure smells good in here." Our chili simmered on the stove. "Haven't eaten since breakfast. Think I could I have a bite before I walk out to the hi-way?" Karen and I exchange a quick look. Then I give him a hot bowl of chili and set a loaf of bread on the table.

"This trouble with the truck couldn't have happened at a worse time." His filthy hands shovel bread and chili into his mouth. "I got a wife and two kids living in a shack. I been cutting wood to put food on the table but without my truck... I needed to sell this wood to buy groceries. Didn't get a moose last fall. Kids can't live on macaroni every day. You need some wood?" He'd seen the remains of our woodpile on his way in.

"How much?" I ask.

"Hundred dollars a cord. And we'll stack it for ya." Woodcutters are notorious for being crooked and unreliable. It's the last resort of a desperate man. But I write a cheque and hand it to him.

"Thanks! We'll eat this week," he says, stuffing my cheque in his pocket. "My buddy and I will unload the wood and stack it when the tow-truck comes tomorrow. Joe's out in the truck. Can he come in and warm up before we hitch to Whitehorse?" If we don't invite him in, he could let himself in with his boot. He's half frozen and ravenous. The two of them finish the chili and the loaf of bread. I put more wood in the stove. "Well, thanks. Guess we should head out. Gotta get home to the family." It's 9:00 pm and stormy, minus 40 degrees and five kilometers to the hi-way where no one will be driving tonight. "Think you could give us a lift to the turn-off? Sure would help us out." The other guy is silent, looks pathetic, exhausted. We both know they could kill us, steal the car and drive to Vancouver before anyone would know. We both know that someone has to stay and tend the fire. Would we expect help from a stranger?

"I'll call you when I get to Whitehorse," Karen says, closing the door behind her before I can move.

It is dark out here. Silent. In town, I crave the quiet. Now, I bolt the door and watch the clock. My lover is out on the frozen hi-way with two men whom we don't know. From our cabin, it's a 40 minute drive to Whitehorse, and 40 minutes to get home – if a gravel truck doesn't send her car into the ditch. I stop myself from pacing by boiling water and washing the dishes. Finally, the phone rings. "Put another log on the fire," my lover croons.

Our bed is warm when she gets home. When the bank opens, my cheque clears. The truck sits there, imposing a deep rut in our driveway. I leave messages for *Family Man* - his long distance call being on my phone bill. Then one day, the truck is gone. So is the wood. Six weeks and $100 in Small Claims Court later, there's a jumble of wood in the driveway. Green as a tree frog. Useless to me as the cops were to Krystal.

The Transition Home is now a fortress of bulletproof glass. Ron Bax is still at large.

Our Pam's Gone Funny

Paddy St. Loe

"Our Pam's gone funny," said my sister-in-law in the midst of a family get together.

"Funny like how?" I inquired.

"Well, she dumped useless Larry last year, and she seems to have taken up with this Erica woman."

"You mean she's become a lesbian?"

"Oh, I didn't say that," replied Gillian hastily. "Oh, I don't really know. We're all just going along with it. She insists that if Erica isn't invited to things she won't come. Everyone's polite, but nobody's asking, if you know what I mean."

I did know what she meant. I hadn't been home for years and found I was now part of the older generation. My parents and most of my aunts and uncles were gone. The ones that remained weren't thinking too clearly. I had been quite an out lesbian at home in Canada for some eight years. It had been my hope that my generation of cousins would be more accepting, and that I could reveal myself to a more enlightened bunch. Not so apparently. There was Cousin Pam living her life out loud, and no one was prepared to talk about it. I was definitely going to have to have a visit. Perhaps she was the one I could come out to first; she'd be able to tell me how the wind was blowing queer-wise.

I found a seat beside Pam and Erica and did the how-do-you-dos while clutching a glass of plonk and plate of nibblies. "I don't think I've met you before," I said to Erica.

"No you wouldn't have. We've only known each other a year."

"I'd love to have a proper visit with you before I go back to Canada," I said.

Hum…I'd said *you* - that could mean Pam or *you both*. That wasn't too clear.

Fortunately it didn't matter. "We'd love to have you! How about Saturday lunch?"

I turned up clutching a loaf of *good bread*, as instructed. I had decided to jump straight in and announce my lesbianism. If I was way off course I could always get up and leave. They beat me to it. "You do know you've entered a den of iniquity and will surely go to hell if you hang out with us?" announced Pam.

I chickened out. "What do you mean?" I said faintly.

'You've been home the better part of a week and visited with the relatives - surely someone's mentioned us?"

"Well, only Gillie. She said you'd dumped Larry and *gone funny.*"

"That about sums it up. None of them want to know. At gatherings they're all polite, but visits and invitations have just about dried up."

"What would happen if you just announced it - I'm taking it that you are lesbian -at the next family do'?

"We talked about it and decided that it would spoil whatever event was going on."

"They'd have to take a position then though, one way or the other," Erica said. "Personally I don't give a damn, yet I've come to like the ones I do know."

"And really," Pam added, "Do we care that much? So what if the family splits over it? Maybe it's better they all stay in blissful willful ignorance than have to face up to something threatening."

"Typically British" was my take on it.

"You seem fine with us," queried Pam.

"It takes one to know one," I said.

I told them I'd had every intention of coming out on this visit and had hoped for a more liberal acceptance. They both wondered where I'd got that idea. I had to admit it was from the British comedies I watched on TV home in Canada. I was told that there was a UK law that said if you portray community on screen, then it must represent all sections of the community. So if I saw gays, it wasn't necessarily because they were an important part of the plot. They cited *Coronation Street* as their example.

I left and we vowed to keep in touch.

So what was I to do now? Come out to one person? The logical choice would be Gillie. She had been my friend, and I had married her brother. She accepted our divorce – had got divorced herself. But how could I tell her I had divorced her brother, a decent and funny man, and left him with no one because I'd realized I was a lesbian? I hadn't told her brother that. The reason I'd given for wanting a divorce was that I wished to leave our small town now that the girls were launched. He, on the other hand, was content to settle down even further.

If I was thinking to tell Gillie, expecting that she in turn would inform the family as and when, then she wasn't really the one to do it. I had to all intents and purposes abandoned her brother for another life. And, for her to be told later by some other member of the family, when I'd been staying in her house, wasn't really on. Pam and Erica would no more out me that I would out them. The family was constrained in their presence but basically would be fine until someone actually came out with the word *lesbians*! If I came out maybe I'd precipitate that very thing, and Pam and Erica weren't prepared to *flaunt it*. They had decided to go along as they were. I'd be long gone back to Canada, and they might well be left with a family divided in their acceptance of them.

So I ended up returning home to my *other* life, despite my earnest intentions about coming out. I still think of this from time to time. Revise all the what ifs. Was there also a measure of lacking the courage to actually do the coming out bit? Was I afraid to face people's reaction?

I'll never know now, but I wonder.

Long Distance

Stephen Hardy

1999

He sat in his royal blue plush velvet chair, one arm strung over the back. He was staring at my crotch.

"How about a drink?" he said.

"No, I'd better not."

"How are you going to relax, calm down, without a drink?"

It was our first date, just after I moved to Vancouver's West End. We had seen the new Canadian movie *New Waterford Girl*, about a young woman trapped in a maritime town, desperate to leave. But the best part of it was the performance by Ashley MacIsaac, the wild rock and roll fiddler from Nova Scotia. Wild, flamboyant Ashley. Wild, outrageously gay Ashley. Protégé of Philip Glass. But more well known for his outrageous flamboyance, his recurring scandals involving younger gay men. Yes, definitely Ashley was the highlight. He had no fear. He had no anxieties. He just lived his gay life, as out and gay as he wanted to be, and fucked whoever wanted to, and whenever opportunities appeared. He showed me what was possible, what there could be for me… if I were free.

"How about that drink now?" he said. "I'd really like it if you stayed awhile. I could show you my place. Maybe give you a massage." My shoulders and neck tensed up. My throat got very tight. I didn't say anything. I couldn't say anything. The old fears were all rushing in again.

He was still staring at my crotch.

Why can't I relax? I thought to myself. *Why can't I trust him? Why can't I trust anyone? What am I afraid of?* I felt as if I was in danger if anyone got close to me, as if I might die, as if I might be killed! *Why can't I trust anyone? Why do I only feel safe when I'm alone?*

My mind drifted back to the old memories - the early ones that seemed to be the start of it all, the start of all the fears. I started to remember, to replay the old memories in my mind...

1951

The boy sat on the carpeted stairs leading to the upstairs bedrooms. The stairway was very dark, as it always was on these lonely winter evenings, this late winter evening. He looked down towards the dark maroon curtains, and through them to the dimly lit front hallway. The boy's uncle sat at the small telephone chair, next to the black telephone on the wall.

The uncle sat, puzzling over the telephone and the long distance instructions in the slim, well-worn, telephone book. The frown on his face, and the puzzled, frustrated expression in his voice became more intense as he dialed the operator.

"I want to call a Bob Hardy in Montreal. No. He's at a hotel. Here it is, the Queen Elizabeth...here's his number."

The boy waited a long time, in anticipation of what his uncle would say, as he seemed overwhelmed by the task of contacting the boy's father. Finally, his uncle spoke.

"Bob," said the uncle. "Is that you?"

"Bob. We've got some good news! It's a girl."

****

The little Austin Hillman sputtered around the corner towards the back of the hospital wing as the three boys looked around in wonder.

"Albert, drive around back here," said the housekeeper to her husband.

"Look, she's in that room. Look, boys! Can you see your mother? Can you see your new sister?"

The oldest boy looked out through the frosted car window over towards the hospital annex. He could see a dim outline through one hospital window but did not recognize it as his mother.

This isn't right, he was thinking. *Why are we not just going into the hospital? Why are we sneaking around the back?*

"Wait here, I'll be able to sneak it in the window," said the housekeeper's husband.

"Oh, Albert! You're not going to do that again, are you? Not at a time like this!"

Albert ran over towards the hospital window carrying a brown paper bag. The boy recognized it as the kind that Albert frequently brought over late in the day, when he picked up his wife. He knew that his mother liked the bottles he brought, and that his mother and Albert often drank from the bottles together.

In a few minutes, Albert came back. "I did it," he said. "The nurse didn't see a thing."

****

The boy stood beside the new crib, looking at his mother trying to bottle feed the baby. She was still normal. She had not become crazy since the baby had come home one week ago, except for a few days at first. The boy wondered about the baby and what she would be like when she grew older.

The boy listened as his mother explained that the baby was named after his aunt Eva. His mother seemed cold and preoccupied, as if she was worrying about something. She often seemed this way when she was normal, just before the craziness would start again. The baby sneezed.

"Oh, baby, do you have a little cold? Stay away from the crib, boys, so the baby doesn't get your colds."

****

The boy's mother was standing in the hallway, holding the baby in her arms. She was different now. She was unsteady, trying to keep her balance. Her face was different, eyelids drooping, cheeks sagging. She was slurring her words. She was really crazy now, crazy and dangerous.

The boy looked up at his mother and thought to himself *She's gone crazy again. I hoped and prayed this wouldn't happen anymore. Not after the baby!*"

The boy's throat became tight, his muscles tensed.

And the baby, the baby is in danger!

****

The boy awoke earlier than usual this morning. He got out of bed and went out to the bookshelf in the hallway. The house was strangely quiet. His father had left again, had driven to the airport a few days earlier, for one of his many business trips.

His mother's other personality, the crazy one, had appeared again. The boy was lonely and scared.

He picked up one of the adventure comic books from the shelf. He liked these comics, with their fantastic stories. He liked burying himself in them. The fictional tension of the story made him forget about the fear and worry he always felt, made the tense feelings seem like fun, at least for a while.

Slowly, the boy became aware of some muffled sounds from his mother's bedroom, like a soft crying. It was a sound he had never heard before, high soft crying, like a baby, but too loud for little Eva. Then, his mother came rushing from the bedroom, carrying the baby.

It was his mother that was crying. It was a sound he had never heard before from his mother, high pitched, desperate, tortured, hopeless, and very, very sad. It had none of the cynical, sarcastic tone that she had when she was in her crazy personality, and it was not cold and unfeeling as in her normal personality. She seemed to be wanting desperately to undo something that was very, very sad, her emotions twisting in every way to try to undo something, but knowing that it was hopeless.

"Oh no! Oh no! I've killed my baby. I've killed my baby."

She kept repeating these words, in the same awful way, as she ran down the stairs towards the telephone.

The boy was very, very scared now. He wondered what would finally happen now? Would his mother stay forever in this state of craziness? Was the baby really dead, or was this just another one of her crazy hallucinations? What would become of him and his brothers now?

****

The doctor was talking to the housekeeper.

"So there's just the oldest in school. You'd better keep him home today. It's going to be hardest on him anyway. I've given his mother a shot; she'll sleep the rest of the day. How much has she been drinking?"

****

The housekeeper took the boy aside.

"The doctor told me the baby died of pneumonia. She had a little cold for the last few days."

"But what was she saying when she ran out of the bedroom? It sounded like she said she had killed the baby."

"She just thought that. She was very upset and hasn't been feeling well these last few days. She'll sleep the rest of the day. I've put all the baby things in the storeroom downstairs, so there will be nothing to remind her of this."

The boy wondered if the doctor's statement was just to make everyone feel better. He wondered why everything had to be hidden, with all the baby things hidden away in the basement storeroom. He felt cold and empty. There was no one anymore. Just the fear was left. He knew his mother was dangerous. He knew he had to stay away from her when she was crazy. Now, he knew just how dangerous she was. The coldness and emptiness enveloped him, a grey cloud with nothing else. He knew now that there was no one to take care of him, no one he could trust.

****

The boy sat on the carpeted stairs leading to the upstairs bedrooms. The stairway was very dark, as always on these lonely winter evenings. He looked down towards the dark maroon curtains and through them to the dimly lit front hallway. The boy's uncle sat at the small telephone chair, next to the black telephone on the wall.

The boy felt cold, felt alone, as if something with hope had just ended, just been finished, with nothing left now but the feelings of hopelessness, emptiness, and fear. The chance for a change in his mother's craziness and in his own helpless and anxious feelings was gone.

The uncle sat, again puzzling over the telephone and the long distance instructions in the slim, well worn, telephone book. The frown on his face and the puzzled, frustrated expression in his voice became more intense as he dialed the operator.

"I want to call a Bob Hardy in Ottawa. No, he's at a hotel. Here it is - the Chateau Laurier. Here's his number."

The boy waited a long time, in anticipation of what his uncle would say, as he seemed overwhelmed by the task of contacting the boy's father. Finally, his uncle spoke.

"Bob, is that you?"

"Bob, we've got some bad news…"

1999

"Sorry, I didn't hear you. Did you say you wanted that drink now? Stay for awhile?"

"No, I can't. I really have to go now. I'm feeling kind of messed up just now. I have to go. Now!"

"Well, OK, maybe some other time then. OK?"

"Sure. Maybe some other time…"

Becoming Woman

Gayle Roberts

"Excuse me ma'am, would you like a seat?"

The overly full bus with its standing passengers squeezed tightly together in the aisle continued its headlong evening rush-hour dash along Granville Street towards the suburbs. It was mid November, dark, cold and, as is typical for Vancouver at that time of year, pouring with rain. Could the unknown speaker be referring to me, I wondered, as I stood in the relative spaciousness of the stairwell, hoping that the question was directed towards someone else. I placed my handbag and still dripping umbrella on the floor while trying to see through fogged glasses if there were any women standing near me. Unfortunately, as I looked around over the top of my glasses, I could see only men who, like me, were desperately trying to maintain their balance as the bus swayed back and forth while sending huge waves of water from the rivers that ran down the street onto pedestrians foolishly standing too close to the curb. I wondered if the speaker would assume I couldn't hear him over the passengers shouting at their friends as they tried to compete with all the noise.

"Excuse me ma'am, would you like a seat?" the voice repeated, but this time there was a gentle tapping on my arm that couldn't be ignored. I turned around to see a man seated next to the stairwell, probably in his mid seventies, looking up at me and smiling. My first thought was that he was old enough to be my father. And then, almost immediately, I felt like an impostor. As I blankly stared into the old man's face, my mind replayed the conversation I'd had only a few hours earlier with my wife about the wisdom of taking my first bus ride ever as a woman.

"Do you think it's a good idea?" she had asked. "Up to now, you've taken the car for your electrolysis appointments."

"That's exactly why I need to take the bus; it's time to give up my security blanket," I said as I recalled wondering whether I would pass as a woman and how people would react to me if I didn't.

Then my mind was brought back to the present as the old man continued. "I just thought you looked as if you could use a seat."

Why couldn't this bus ride be like the one into town? When I had gotten onto the bus a few passengers had looked up at me and then turned to look out the windows or back to their reading as I walked past them. The passengers who had boarded the bus after me seemed not to have seen me at all. Even the lady who had sat down next to me had ignored me as she folded her umbrella, placed it on the floor, and stared out of the window.

"I hope you don't mind me saying it, but you look soaked to the skin," the old man said.

Would he think I was a man as soon as I spoke? What about the other passengers; would they know? Then I realized that the longer I took to answer the old man's question, the greater the likelihood that I would draw attention to myself. "That's very kind of you," I said in as high a pitched voice as I could. We exchanged places and I added, "I think you're right about me being soaked."

"Well, your shoes and the bottom of your slacks are certainly wet enough," he said.

"Thank you for offering me your seat. Not many people do that these days. Especially children," I said, as I looked at some boisterous high school students seated across the aisle from me.

"When I was a boy, my parents taught me to give up my seat to adults and that when I became a man, I should give up my seat to women," the old man said.

"And you continue to do that now?" I said.

"Not all the time. When I was a boy, I always did without giving it a second thought. My parents expected me to do that, and I simply did it. But as I got older, I started asking myself why each of us should simply blindly follow society's expectations. Do you know what I do now?" the old man asked. I shook my head and he continued, "I think about how sensible the expectations are. I offered you my seat because you looked like you needed it. It was as simple as that. It doesn't matter to me whether you're a man or a woman; you just looked like someone who could use a rest." As he spoke, the bus lit up as we entered the tunnel, "The other reason I offered you my seat was that it makes me feel good. Sometimes, I give up my seat to other men and occasionally even to children if I see a need. You'd be surprised at some of the interesting conversations I've had."

The bus, as suddenly as it had become bright, plunged back into darkness again, "I normally love it when we come out of the tunnel into the farmland," I said. "The openness gives me a feeling of freedom, but it's so dark there's nothing to see."

"True," the old man said, "but you know those fields are there even though you can't see them. Tomorrow, they'll be in daylight - fresh and green." The old man zipped up his rain jacket and pulled its waterproof hood over his head.

"Are you getting off here?" I asked.

"I have to transfer to the other bus at Ladner Trunk Road. I expect you're carrying on?"

"Yes," I replied as the old man stepped through the open doors of the bus, "I'm carrying on."

I stared out of the window at the blackness and the reflection of a woman.

About the 2000s and 2010s

Elise Chenier

If you came of age in the 2000s, you might have been able to join a gay-straight alliance at school, it's possible that your parents knew you were gay before you did, and your prom king or queen could have been, well, a queen. You had easy access to gay literature, you could take in any number of gay-themed movies at the annual queer film festival, and you could even watch *Will and Grace* on television every night, with your siblings beside you. At the dawn of the new century, it seemed that most every barrier had come down. (Trans* people, whose experiences and issues are distinct from lesbians and gays, were only just beginning to become part of the dialogue). In 2003, same-sex marriage rights were won, leaving just about every battle safely behind us. What was left but to settle down with the perfect partner, buy a house, and subscribe to Gayble TV?

This final section reminds us that life's challenges never cease. It reveals how a lifetime of struggle equips us with the insight, wisdom, compassion, and strength we need to get ourselves and our loved ones through. It also reminds us that people never stop fighting for the right to live how they want to, not even in 'old age,' a phrase that some of these writers scoff at while others negotiate it with great care.

We would do well to remember that it was a couple in their 'old age' who knocked down the first domino that ultimately led to the changes that culminated with same-sex marriage. Jim Egan and John Norris Nesbit began living together in 1948. As a young man in the 1950s, Egan sustained an active letter-writing campaign that challenged news media depictions of homosexuals as perverted and depraved. He was, in short, a gay activist in Canada at a time when 'gay rights' was a dream imagined only by the few. When Egan turned sixty-five, he began collecting Old Age Pension. When his partner reached the same age, he applied to the Department of National Health and Welfare for a spousal allowance. He was refused on the basis that the definition of spouse did not include a member of the same sex. And so their court battle began.

Nesbit and Egan challenged the Canadian government to extend the Charter of Rights and Freedoms to include protection against discrimination based on sexual orientation. Their victory in the courts led to the quick dismantling of every legal barrier that kept lesbians and gays from enjoying the same citizenship rights as their heterosexual counterparts. In this section, Paula Stromberg reminds us that in the preceding decades lesbians and gays could not openly mourn the loss of a lover. Today we can apply for paid bereavement leave. Stromberg also shows us that while not every lesbian and gay person was eager to marry once they had the right to do so in 2003, at least one seventy-seven year old grabbed that brass ring as soon as it came within reach. Not only that, by marrying a woman much younger than herself she shows us that one never has to stop living just as one pleases, that the lessons -- and lifestyles -- of the past are not soon forgotten.

Lesbian and gay couples could also now adopt children *as a couple*. Change happens slowly in some places, but overall forming families became 'normal' and was not something one necessarily had to hide. As Bridget Coll shows in her story about 'chosen families,' these exciting changes left a lot of folks having to catch up and learn things they had not learned before, such as how to diaper and feed a baby. Though families of origin might now be easier to sustain relations with, the chosen family lives on, and lives strong.

The challenges of aging are equally profound for trans* people. Those who struggled for legal and social gains in the 1980s and 1990s have paved the way for younger generations. Anti-discrimination protection based on gender has yet to be extended to Canadians, but efforts to see such a bill through continue. Political movements in support of queer rights are no longer dominated by youth. Advocacy, organization, and support come from all age groups.

As stories in this collection show, political battles for dignity and equality evolve from our most intimate and private experiences. These stories are tools we use to heal ourselves, and to build communities. With stories, we make a livable life possible.

This collection ends with Maggie Shore's *Shards and Scree,* a poem that captures the fragile nature of memory and poses a difficult question: if I can't remember my own thoughts, do I exist? By laying down one's life in words, we can all know again and remember once more the way profound social changes touch and transform individual life, and the way individual lives lived lead to profound social changes. Many of the experiences put down here may not be ones we ourselves have had, but we all have lived, in some way or another, on the stage of historical change. What the events of our lives mean to us changes as we grow older. What once seemed so essential diminishes in importance, and other priorities take their place. The writers in this collection have lived through difficult and dangerous times, and they show us that the battles never end, they just change. After a lifetime of swimming against the current, they remain strong. And in sharing their stories, we, too, grow in strength.

It Takes Balls

River Glen

Forget It!

Nancy Strider

Worse than the mistake is that I can't remember making it.
Cash went short in the shared till. I'd done the lunchtime watch.
The young cashier assumes I gave the same change twice.
The customer, when asked, supported me. But Cashier says:
   Of course she'd lie.

No surveillance video, but my mental replay shows no glitches.
Fingered, I push back firmly: *I have no recollection that I did that.*
I offer re-enactment, but he says: *Now you'd do it right.*
Of course you could have slipped, and then forgot.

What's happening to my access to reasonable doubt?
Lack of a memory could be proof, or just a small black hole.
Slashed by his Occam's razor, I still refuse the simplest logic.
But my fear -- of withering neurons -- looks like shame.

Seeing me on the run, he shrugs. *Forget it. Just move on.*
But have I now become the usual suspect?
Is it time to start a notebook, like my Dad's?
Am I shape-shifting from an Us into a Them?

The Strength to Get Old

River Glen

9:50 pm

It was a pillow top mattress. The sheets were high thread count, and RJ's special pillow cradled her neck and head. The room around her was adorned with her special things: her childhood teddy bear, threadbare and fast asleep on Grandma's rocking chair, art made by the kids when they were little. Daisy snored gently on her purple satin pillow. RJ set the book down on the bedside table and switched off the lamp.

Pain jerked up its lowered head and pulled the reins out of her hands. It wasn't fair. RJ had spent the waking hours making sure she cooked and ate well, did the chores, exercised, and reached out to others through the Internet. She had rested with reading, TV, and some embroidery. She didn't deserve a seven-year sentence with Fibromyalgia as a cellmate. Nerves fired at random. She tried turning on her right side, then her left, then back, able to endure the pressure on her burning skin for only moments at a time. Time was suspended as all the other nights of insomnia blurred into this one. Her legs could have bicycled across town, but there was nowhere to go and no place to hide. An occasional sharp acute spasm radiated out of her neck or in the groin or from her heart. Crazy migrating shocks made her breath catch in her throat.

10:50 pm

RJ was tucked into a fetal position; only her toes, knees, elbows and forehead touched the bedding. Worries chased their own tails down all the dead ends of the labyrinth in her head. Insomnia and FM were seeds sown during the early years of a long life. Even as a child she'd spent nights of coughing herself blue in the face from undiagnosed allergy/asthma from ubiquitous cigarette smoke. At age ten she'd been up in the middle of the night watching Nelson Eddie and Jeanette Mac-Donald during the few days it took her appendix to rupture. Then there was the self-induced follies of psychedelic tripping in the sixties and booze and coke marathons in the seventies. The eighties brought the babies - a good six years of wakeful nights. The nineties were an endurance test - divorce, university all nighters, and four teenagers, money problems, coming out, life long crazies, OCD and depression. Her new career in Social Work seemed totally unreal until a bad virus and the full on onset of fibromyalgia insisted she never forget to look after herself again.

RJ turned onto her back, opened her palms and counted breaths. Flex and relax. Feet. Legs. Body. Shut up, Monkey. We're breathing. She told herself the story of the garden with the waterfall, birdsong, and fluffy clouds floating through the sky.

She screamed silently inside.

She wondered if just maybe it was time to take a sleeping pill in addition to the Melatonin and script stuff.

12:15 am

Daisy looked at RJ with practiced incredulity, then re-tucked herself into a furry ball. RJ got up and peed. She would do that twice more during the next seven hours of various stages of sleep, sweat, chill, and dark dreams.

7:20 am

In a trying day of pain, clumsiness, and forgetfulness, RJ recollected how little sleep she could get by on when she had youth and vitality.

1:30 pm

A pleasant peaceful drowsiness flowed over her diluting pain. Blessed with no pressing obligations, RJ opened herself to the experience. She tucked Daisy under her arm and floated back to her bed, which magically change from a rack of torture to a place of comfort as she slid between the sheets.

3:30 pm

RJ woke with a feeling near to wellbeing, her aches and pains reduced to background noise. A small simple miracle.

"This is the definition of happiness," she told her dog.

There was food in the fridge. It had stopped pouring rain, and there was a friendly email in the inbox.

When she was so young vital and life was such drama, why didn't she know how much happiness was all around her?

It's not my 77th birthday. We got married

Paula Stromberg

Same-sex marriage became legal on July 8, 2003, in British Columbia, the second region in Canada and North America to pass such a law. Just a few months later, my sailor friend Butters, a then 77-year old lesbian who lives on the Gulf Islands, left an unforgettable message on my answering machine. Don't imagine that being 77-years old renders Butters feeble. She teaches chainsaw graffiti and has lived her achievement-filled life in fierce resistance to ageism and sexism. Woe betide those who dare ask her age, question her May-December relationship, or treat older lesbians as invisible. And if you are her friend, you dare not phone her on her birthday. Butters shouts at misguided well-wishers, "Don't call me on my birthday. It's depressing. Who wants to be reminded you're one step closer to that?" Knowing her birthday had just passed, I was surprised to see Butters' message blinking on my answering machine...

"Oh, too bad. It's your voice mail. We're calling with some news. We just sailed home and want you to know we got married Monday. We didn't want a fuss. Just four of us were there. We went to a nice justice of the peace — female — with our friends Sara and Betty on Saturna Island. Eighteen years living together, and now we're married. No family, nobody knew. When our island friends act shocked at our news, we tell 'em we couldn't invite a soul on Pender for fear we'd leave somebody out.

"But you know, we really kept quiet we were getting married 'cause we didn't want to discuss it. Not everybody, even in our own lesbian community, agrees with this marriage business. But I don't want to hear all those opinions. I don't care.

"And you know, some of my older friends are embarrassed to hear about *gay*. When we were young, you'd never admit openly or say so-and-so was your lover. It just wasn't done. Even if there was a funeral, it was just "Oh, my friend died." The word lesbian was shameful. We covered it up. I was like that 'til I got with Louise 18 years ago. She made me change, got all that out of me.

"Believe me, I had a lot of changing to do back when we first got together - being 59 with a 29-year-old lover. Louise. Oh boy, when we fell in love, we were the scandal of the inlet. Lots of my friends wouldn't talk to me, taking up with a hippie artist half my age. And a proud lesbian at that. So beautiful she turned heads everywhere. Ha! I liked makin' people jealous.

"Now society's changed. Getting married is my right. You might not understand now, but back then we felt dirty. That's hard to shake. So now the law changed, you bet I got married."

Adopted Grammas

Bridget Coll

I am not a parent, but I am a grandparent.

I never thought I would be called Gramma Bridget until I discovered a hairdresser on Commercial Drive. I discovered to my delight that she is a lesbian (this was the first time that I had met a lesbian who was pregnant).

On one of my visits, she told me that she was leaving the hairdressing salon because she did not want the child she was carrying to be affected by the chemicals that were being used there. She invited my partner, Chris, and me to her home and said that if we wished, she would continue to be our hairdresser. A few months later, she invited us to a baby shower, where, to our surprise, she announced that we were to be the grammas.

On December 18th, I came home from work and listened to our phone messages. One said, "Colleen was born at twelve minutes after six this morning."

I said to Chris, "I think we should go and see this child since we are the Grammas." We saw this tiny child, held her, and fell in love with her.

We brought her the classic Pooh Bear, the first of many gifts. We were regular visitors at Colleen's home. We accompanied Colleen to Santa Claus Parades, to St. Patrick's Day Parade and went to her school concerts. In her first pre-school she was "A Little Duck in New York City." She got a standing ovation for that and was happy with her performance. Needless to say, her Grammas were very proud of her, as were her mothers.

When our hairdresser and her partner moved to Bowen Island, we were frequent visitors to our granddaughter's new home. When Colleen was able to talk, she would see us and call out, "Here come the Grammas." When her moms went out together, we babysat and watched every stage of her development. We played with her, and one day we got really excited when she smiled at us, and then even more so when she called us Gramma.

It was a new learning experience to have a child in our lives, and we had a lot to learn. I needed lessons on how to hold, give bottles, and change diapers. After several trials and errors, I became an expert - especially on how to change diapers. In the beginning, I was puzzled about putting diapers on the right way. However, I did learn ever so slowly.

As Colleen's first Christmas approached, Chris and I tried to figure out how to buy a present for her. In the end, we went to Toys R Us and followed women around the store who were accompanied by children the same age as Colleen. We watched to see what toys they played with or begged their mothers to buy. Then we would buy that toy.

Colleen opened up our lives to a whole new experience of nature. She liked to walk around the garden, even in the rain, dressed in a yellow raincoat with Wellingtons to match. She would walk in front of us and every so often, she would bend over, look down and say, "Hi slug."

On her last birthday, Colleen called us and said, "I am now officially nine years old."

What a joy to have such a child in our lives and to be called Grammas!

As I wrote earlier, a child in our lives is a new experience. Now Colleen comes to visit us. She looks around and sees her photos in every room in our house. She looks at us and says, "I know you love me."

We are adopted.

Not the Piece I Was Meant to Write

Christine Waymark

As I look at the straining zippers on the big blue suitcase, I remember the first time I saw her pack. She started with a list, crossing off each item as she put it in its niche.

"I want to be able to manage my luggage by myself. And leave space for treasures I find," she said. Later I learned that stones and driftwood were often part of her trove.

She rolled her socks and tucked them into an inside pocket. "Mum and Dad gave me this suitcase set for my graduation."

"Which one?" I asked, watching her wrap a small flashlight in a handkerchief.

"Oh, my MA. Mum got them at Eaton's with her employee discount."

She put her toothbrush and toothpaste and brush and comb into separate drawstring bags and tied each bag carefully before tucking it into its pocket. In the lid pocket she put underwear and pj's, folded flat so they didn't squash the t-shirts. Slacks and shorts went in the main compartment.

"I haven't seen a Seagram's bags since we used them as purses in High School," I laughed. "I got one from my uncle since dad didn't buy much whisky."

"My parents had plenty," said Robin putting her sandals in one and slippers in another. With a snap she closed the case, locked it, and fastened a leather strap around it.

"Done."

Over the last thirty years, we've travelled many times together. After the first ten, practicality overcame sentiment and Robin packed away her much loved cases and bought a set with wheels. I bought her a rainbow strap, and she retired the old leather one.

"I've written a list for you to go over." I hand it to her.

"What's this for?"

"It's just some suggestions. See I've done one for my packing. Eve will help you tomorrow, after she does the laundry. Remember she did that last time and you said she was really good?"

"Yeah! She folds things really flat."

"Wanna go over the list?"

"Later maybe. I'm tired. I just carried the suitcases upstairs."

On Friday, Eve and Robin pack together and put the suitcase on the couch in the living room. On Sunday, I notice that it looks much fuller. In the outside pocket, I find a National Geographic, three books, her electric toothbrush wrapped in a scarf, an umbrella, and a box of Purdy's chocolates.

I open the case. Two more books are stuffed down the sides of the clothes and two are on top of a jacket. I notice her toiletries bag is too stuffed to close. Gently lifting a few things, I see that at least the neatly packed clothes that Eve helped her with are still there.

Oh Shit! Will she remember what is there? Will she be anxious if I take things out? The new things aren't labeled, as requested by the respite center.

I am so tired. I try to think it through.

Then I take a deep breath, and, with great difficulty, I zip the case.

****

Sunlight bounces from the kitchen counter tops and brick red floor tiles. Bright yellow walls hold the sunbeams. We designed everything for two women who are less than 5' 1". The shelves in the upper cupboards are adjustable, and under the counter are shallow drawers for kitchen tools plus deep drawers holding all the other big stuff a cook accumulates. I cook and Robin cleans up. She's taught me about organizing drawers and cupboards.

When I check the messages on the phone, I hear her familiar voice: "Where are you, and when are you coming back?" By the ninth, she is sounding sad. "I think I might have left a few other messages. But when are you coming home?"

The last message is from Robin's niece. "Hi Christine. Maria here. Just wanted to let you know we took Anna to see Robin yesterday and had a great time. Robin held Anna and even carried her around to meet some of her new friends at the centre. We sent you some pictures."

I start to assemble things to make a pie for Robin's homecoming. Flour, salt, shortening…whoops! Where's the bowl?

I open the drawer with the Tupperware containers. Nope. I look in the pan drawer. Nope. Nope. Nope.

Okay! I'll get the measuring cups and spoons. Oh damn! Can't find them either, but I do find the phone charger I've been trying to find for weeks. Tears flow as I go through the drawers returning vagrant items to their places.

The aroma of apricot cherry pie fills the kitchen.

Tomorrow she'll be home.

And I'll still be missing her.

Wrinkles

Marsha Ablowitz

I sometimes imagine my life was a clean sheet of paper at my birth, or maybe a clean diaper, or better yet a new road map neatly laid out including my major life events: birth, Hebrew school, ballet lessons, tree climbing, Zionist summer camp, strapless grad gown, kibbutz in Israel, university, snotty Jewish sorority to catch a nice Jewish Lawyer or Doctor, join the matrons monthly Hadassah meetings with every hair in place.

If that was my roadmap, it started wrinkling from the very start. I never got the ballet moves right, could never bend over and gracefully touch my toes. And that coral pink strapless grad gown felt so prickly and uncomfortable, I could hardly move in it. I couldn't sit smiling and listen to those eligible Jewish lawyers when there were revolutions to fight, houses to build, and mountains to climb, and so many cute girls to kiss. Then, somewhere along the way I got hooked on the shining white Himalayas, the thin bright air, the space where mother Ganges got herself tangled in Lord Shiva's wild dreadlocked hair. Shiva dances our dance of life on the mountaintops, and Mother Ganges flows down from those bright icy places. I can't stop my self from hiking back up there, despite the crumbling narrow routes and my trouble breathing in thin air.

By now my road map is as twisted, torn and stained as the Tea Walla's wipe up rag. Down in the foothills at Rishikesh, I sit on the white sandy banks of Mother Ganges, looking back on all those charming women who were my lovers, but not one Jewish husband, not one Hadassah meeting.

My hair is undyed, my face unbotoxed. There are plenty of mountains climbed, and rivers crossed, but no photos of children in my wallet. My outfit is faded; my lover's body is creased and sagging like mine as her warm arms rock me each night by the holy river. Her face lies close to mine, freckled and wrinkled as our two road maps.

Shards and Scree

Maggie Shore

Ellie and Doris smile at each other
across the cafe table, sipping chamomile tea
between tidbits of news,
their white hair two halos of light.

Ellie suddenly brightens over an important
insight about their trip to Reno.
She is preparing to speak
her mouth poised, savoring the taste
of the first words.

A long pause hangs between them.

"Dammit Doris, I had this great idea
I was going to tell you, something about…
and it just went *poof,* disappeared
as if the words had leaped off a cliff
and fallen into darkness."

Doris replies nonchalantly:
"If you don't' use it, you lose it."
and Ellie sniffs into her yellow hanky
dabs her eyes.

She wonders aloud:
"God, Doris, where does that stuff go?
Those unsaid things that just disappear,
a whole sentence formed in your mouth - gone.
It happens to me a lot these days."

"Oh dear," Doris offers. "Don't you worry so."

Ellie continues:
"All those words and ideas -
gone in a flash, dropped into oblivion,
wherever that is. Maybe those lost fragments are just
lying about at the base of the cliff,
piles of dark shards and scree of lost memories."

"Well dear," said Doris, "Maybe they're recycled, who knows?
So let's head back now. You know they don't like it
when we're late for supper."

Biographies

MARSHA ALBOWITZ

Marsha Ablowitz was surprised to wake up one day, aging. Before it was too late, she once again trekked the Himalayas to the source of Mother Ganges and scrambled on the ice slopes of the deeply crevassed Gangotri glacier, which is sadly melting away. She tells this story in "My Roadmap." She describes her loving engulfing Jewish family in the 1950's recoiling from a gay relative in "Max Dexall Gay Pioneer." A social worker, Marsha taught the first all-women's self defense groups, facilitated the first public lesbian support groups and was co-therapist for the first sexual abuse survivors groups in Vancouver. Marsha explores new countries and new mountains and is always happy to come home to her Rainbow City Vancouver. She has over a thousand hits per month on her Hubpages writing site-under the name "marshacanada".

DOUGLAS BACON

Douglas Bacon is a sixty-six year old gay man. In retrospect he realizes he was homosexual in orientation from birth but during his childhood and youth the word 'homosexual' was not in dictionaries let alone in common parlance. As a Protestant minister he was a constant advocate for marginalized persons (e.g.: refugees, native Canadians, mentally-ill, imprisoned, LGTBs, women, men and children in poverty). When he was fifty-one he became an advocate for the identity he had marginalized in himself: gay, artistic, loveable. His advocacy for himself and others continues to be his passion.

KELSEY BLAIR

Kelsey Blair joined Quirk-e as an Assistant Artist in 2010 and is currently Co-Lead Artist with Claire Robson. She is a writer, director, and former female professional basketball player. Kelsey holds an M.A. in Cinema Studies from the University of Toronto and is currently pursuing an MA in Theatre Studies from the University of British Columbia. She likes her coffee black, her tea herbal and her strawberries in all forms but jelly.

GWYNETH BOWEN

Gwyneth, at 63, is finding life still continually brings new joys, one of them being a member of the Quirk-e collective, and invitations to metamorphosis. Her earlier evolutions include becoming (and this is the short list) a mother of two daughters (one queer), bringing her treasures untellable; a therapist who works with women healing from abuse, teaching her deep respect and humility; a gardener, resulting in dirty fingernails, joy, and peace; a late life lesbian, opening the door to new love and a rich community; and a show-off in male or female drag, offering up serious goofiness at the tip of a fedora. She demands the prize for the longest sentence. She wonders, what's next?

JANIE CAWLEY

I was born in 1947. I was everything my parents hoped I would be until 1982 when I left my marriage and announced I was a lesbian. Many then believed that being a lesbian was incompatible with being a mother. I found myself fighting a custody battle over who would be the better parent: the man who beat his wife or the lesbian. My children and I still have scars from that battle, but the repatriation of the Constitution and Charter of Rights decisions that followed have made some things better. My same sex marriage is a testament to that.

ELISE CHENIER

Elise Chenier is a historian who teaches and researches at Simon Fraser University in Burnaby, BC, Canada. She works on various aspects of the history of sexuality in the modern world, and is currently writing a book on same-sex marriage in the 1950s, 60s and 70s. Elise is also the director of the Archives of Lesbian Oral Testimony (A LOT) www.alotarchives.org

BRIDGET COLL

As far back as Bridget can remember she was taught that she was a Catholic. She learned that there were laws, rules and commandments that she was expected to obey without question. If she failed to comply there would be punishments, if not in this life then in the hereafter. When she grew up Bridget learned that society had laws and rules also that had to be obeyed. There would also be consequences and punishments if she did not comply to those laws and rules. When she realized that she was a lesbian and her way of life would be frowned on by society she decided to keep a low profile and be like the heterosexual world she lived in. When she came to Canada her Canadian partner applied to Immigration to sponsor her as her same-sex partner. In no uncertain terms Canadian Immigration informed her that there was no such category in Canadian law. Her partner then filed a suit in federal court alleging discrimination on the basis of sexual orientation and founded an organization that worked to change the law to include same-sex partners. Bridget and her partner along with other same –sex partners worked for 10 years until the law was changed in July 2002 to include same-sex partners in the Family Class.

JUDY FLETCHER

When Judy Fletcher was growing up in rural Ontario in the 1950s and 1960s no one talked about homosexuality unless it was behind the barn or in the pool hall. She got an education and found her way to the big city. While most of her peers married and had children, she still had no words for why she was not attracted to men. Fiercely fighting for her independence and battling mental illness was all there was energy for, until one day, when she was almost too old to care, Judy found herself with a major crush on a woman.

FARREN GILLASPIE

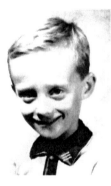

Farren grew up on a farm in Ontario, smothered by Baptist and Catholic ideals. He escaped at seventeen to live on his own. Plunged into the seventies armed with psychedelics and left the seventies a meditating vegetarian. Once the fog cleared he came out as gay rather than bisexual. Moved to Calgary where he co-founded a very successful gay camping group. After two holidays in Vancouver moved here.

Continued career working with the disabled. Pursued alternative health modalities, including herbs, nutrition and training as a Reiki Master. Lived on Bowen Island while leading men's groups for ACOA and groups for people dealing with HIV. Supported several friends through their final transition. Discovered a seventeen year old daughter when he was thirty-nine. At forty-six lost a partner to hepatitis. Shortly after fiftieth birthday met a special man who has been his current partner ever since. Now he wants to share his experiences through his writing while at the same time evolve as the quiet gardener.

RIVER GLEN

River Glen celebrates her involvement with Quirk-e and her participation in the Queer community in Vancouver and Kelowna British Columbia. She holds a Bachelor of Social Work and has four successful adult children. River has lived with the mental illness, survived cancer and for a decade chronic pain. She first became an ally of her gay friends in high school only to spend most of her adult life trying to fit into the straight world. Fifteen years ago River left her marriage and fully embraced the LGBT culture. Her writing explores injustice, inequality and the challenges of aging well.

STEPHEN HARDY

Dr. Hardy graduated from the University of Alberta in 1971 with a Ph.D. in Electrical Engineering. He subsequently worked in both industry and academia for close to forty years, retiring in 2010 to a position of Professor Emeritus at Simon Fraser University, Canada.

Dr. Hardy was employed by the University of Saskatchewan, the University of Regina, University of British Columbia, and Simon Fraser University. He also worked at the Saskatchewan Power Corporation R&D Centre, the BC Microelectronics Society, and worked as a consultant for many electrical and electronics firms in western Canada. Dr. Hardy has been a registered Professional Engineer in Alberta and Saskatchewan and currently in British Columbia. Dr. Hardy struggled with anxiety and depression throughout much of his life, but was to a great extent unaware of the basis of this struggle, until he finally "came out" and lived in solidarity with gay people in the final 10 years of his career.

PAT HOGAN

As a child in Putnam Connecticut, Pat considered becoming an acrobatic nun, influenced by the film, "The Flying Nun", her Catholic upbringing, and futile attempts to do a perfect cartwheel for cheerleader try-outs. Moving on to Manhattan, San Francisco, and Canada she has packed in a lifetime of social activism and community organization. She has supported herself, and raised her two kids by dint of her administrative and entrepreneurial skills. Pat enjoys being in the thick of things and says she will remain there until she drops in the box.

Although she scrambles to meet deadlines, Pat will always have time for family and friends. Life is precious and NOW is really all that matters.

GRETA HURST

Greta Hurst was on her way to Germany in 1939 where her German father had been promised an affluent life as the German economy was booming but fortunately for her and her Canadian status, WW II was declared before the family could board the ship. Starting school in the early 40's, she told her first lie, that her father was Norwegian just like her mother. But word must have gotten out by third grade because all the kids turned around to look at her accusingly when the teacher said one boy's fighter pilot father had just been shot down. Life at home was also difficult as mother's Norwegian community was ostracizing her for having a German husband so they were fighting non-stop without actual ammunition. During the 50's, Greta who was finding her voice and being somewhat unconventional discovered that having a lesbian relationship was considered nasty and very deviant.

In the 60's, Greta got married and had three children, now doing what she should have been doing a lot sooner. She then ruined her image by coming out as a lesbian in the 70's which is what "Love in Montreal" is all about. Now 75, she's considering recreating her story to the screen on the lines of the popular "Coronation Street" series and calling it "Coloniale Street" where she lived her childhood in Montreal.

She now knows there's promise of a continuing good life even in old age – just watch her go.

VAL INNES

Val is a transplanted Scot to Winnipeg in 1958, then to the West Coast in '91. A university instructor, with Masters degrees in English and Education, a feminist, a writer, an artist, a builder, who loves winter holidays in warm places and summer holidays at an Ontario Lake, Val values the community and writing combination that Quirke has brought her. She cannot picture a life without politics, without an effort to make the world a better, more equal place, any more than she can picture it without books, without writing, without women or without talk, deep intense talk. She has lived, both personally and professionally, with that politicization as a background, teaching and volunteering in various organizations, as well as protesting and marching, to help bring about positive change.

CHRIS MANN

Chris is the love child of a numbers magician & a songstress who raised her in Montreal. She comes from the farthest galaxy, 5th star from the left. She loves fresh greens, picnics, A.A. Milne, singing loudly everywhere, blackberries, candles, Simon & Garfunkel, curry, finger painting, making snow angels, Christmas stockings, and learning jazz guitar. She has been found guilty of using the exclamation point in abundance! Chris does not play the bagpipes, but wishes she did. All things considered, she most wants to change the world. Or at least get the laundry done. This year she dreams of hiking in the mountains, photographing everything, and living in a state of wonder.

CHRIS MORRISSEY

I was born in England in 1942 to Roman Catholic parents who decided to immigrate to Canada so that me and my two brothers would live better lives and where we would be free to practice our religion. Little did they know! My first quasi-sexual experience with another girl was under the guise of practicing for boys. In 1960, I entered the convent and became a missionary sister. It was many years before I heard the word homosexual and lesbian, despite recognizing my attraction to women. It was wrong. A mortal sin. I would go to hell. Living as a woman in the Catholic Church and under a Chilean dictatorship for the better part of a decade, I learned about oppression, including my own. I left the convent in order to live more congruently. Returning to Canada in 1989, I became an activist; suing the Queen of England and the Minister of Immigration so that my partner and I could live together in Canada. I was part of the December

9th Coalition in which we worked together to bring changes to the laws to end discrimination against LGBT people in Canada. I continue to work both nationally and internationally to bring about justice for all LGBT people.

BILL MORROW

The Sexual History of Bill Morrow

- I was taught to masturbate by a female adult at age 5. This aroused my sexuality. My parents caught me masturbating. Their only sex education was: don't do it.
- In Elementary School, I was sexually curious and by talking with other boys, I learned sex was a sin. Some boys still explored sex with me.
- In High School, I was sexually active. I learned that not only was sex with males a sin, it was perverted.
- By using Gaydar, I found some boys were interested.
- I resolved the sin problem by firing God and deciding never to trust adults.
- In Grade 12, I had my only sex education from adults: a film with no discussion.
- I don't remember it being helpful as there was no discussion about homosexuality. In university, the library had little information about homosexuality except the medical model.

- Homosexuality was natural to me and I tried to fit into the public idea that it was wrong. In hindsight, I used my studies in Psychology and Psychiatry to explore my sexuality.
- I tried to change my sexuality but it didn't work. I accepted that I was closet, active homophobic gay.
- I became involved with Generation's project (Quirke and converted to SGI Buddhism)
- I overcame my homophobia and became free.

SANDRA MUDD

Sandra Mudd emigrated to Canada at 21 because she never felt she belonged in her native country, England. It took her 6 years to understand that she had always been attracted to women and men would simply be friends. During her 42 years in Canada, Sandra has lived in Ontario, Manitoba, Alberta and B.C. She was a founding member of the Gazebo Connection and feels fortunate to live at a time when being gay can be celebrated. She lives in Vancouver just off the Drive with her partner of 6 years. She is semi-retired and learning how not to be a workaholic by writing, singing, travelling, and enjoying life.

CLAIRE ROBSON

Claire Robson is co-lead artist for Quirk-e – the queer imaging & riting kollective for elders. The collective, which has worked under her direction for the last eight years, has made many public shows and presentations, including a human library project and workshops for queer youth and youth leaders. Claire was recently awarded a two-year postdoctoral fellowship by the Social Science and Humanities Research Council of Canada. She is working in the Department of Gender, Sexuality, and Women's Studies and studying arts-engaged community practices. A widely published writer of fiction, memoir, and poetry, Claire's most recent book, Writing for Change, focuses upon the potential of collective memoir writing to effect social change.

ROBIN RENNIE

I am amazed and delighted as the colours
And strands of my life drift, shift, and form anew,
According to the fullness of my dreams.
Time brings the textures of age.
The patterns, like the fractal wrinkles on my face,
Deepen and grow in eternal complexity.
I experience the exquisite beauty of life.
I am full with wonder and gratitude.

GAYLE ROBERTS

Since her transition from male to female in 1995, Gayle Roberts has written several short stories which range from her earliest memories as a gender-variant child in England up to the present. Throughout most of Gayle's life, transsexuality has been perceived by society and the medical profession to be a mental disorder. That awareness caused Gayle (and many other gender-variant people) to live with shame and in fear less her secret inner-being was revealed to the world. For Gayle, as with countless others, the imposed stress caused by a binary gendered society's expectations could not be maintained indefinitely. For peace of mind, she had to transition. Transitioning can be a time of fear. Fear of rejection by loved ones, fear of the loss of a career, fear of physical harm by others and, perhaps the greatest fear, the fear of the unknown. For most of us, those fears are usually short-lived and at last we achieve the inner peace we have sought all our lives. Thankfully, for today's gender-variant children, adolescents and young adults, transphobia is less prevalent in society and, at long last, most (but certainly not all) members of western society and their healthcare workers recognize that gender-variance is simply a normal variation of what it means to be human.

CHRIS SPENCER

Chris did manage to fly away from England in 1968 – she landed in Vancouver in the same year and has never wanted to live anywhere else.

Her passions include food, history, jazz and Brahms.

Her enthusiasm for the Vancouver Canucks is almost equal to that of Everton FC.

The Wizard is no longer in print, alas…

PAULA STROMBERG

Paula Stromberg is an NGO Journalist/ Filmmaker covering women's empowerment, LGBTQ and human rights issues around the world. Her story writing, labour newspapers, photography and art designs have won more than 50 national and international awards over the past several years. **www.paulastromberg.com**

Stromberg's documentaries have been screened in India at an international AIDS conference 2012, in Phnom Penh, Cambodia and circulated among international stakeholders. The movies also screened at SFU Centre for the Arts, Vancouver's BOLD Conference, Saltspring Pride, Red Cross seminars and Against the Grain at Western Front Gallery in Vancouver. Most recently, Stromberg's writing is published in Xtra Newspaper, Xtra.ca and in Mothering Canada Anthology by Demeter Press. Currently Stromberg volunteers as International Coordinator of the Anti-Witchcraft Accusation Coalition of Ghana.

MAGGIE SHORE

I was born in Vancouver in 1935, a time between the two Great Wars. In the 40's, my family lived on a farm in the North Okanogan and I finished my schooling in Armstrong B.C. I worked at various office jobs until 1966. When I spent a year travelling overseas and living in Sydney, Australia. In Vancouver, I earned a 5-year degree in Graphic Design and was employed in this field for 10 years. In 1980, I worked as a Court Recorder in the Vancouver Provincial Courts, retiring in 1988. Presently living in a housing co-op in Kitsilano, my hobbies are music, photography, hiking and periodically clowning in community events.

PADDY ST. LOE

Born at the start of the second world war, Paddy was there in the 70's when feminism was just becoming a realization, There too, in the 80's when equal rights for women and other minorities was the burning issue. Paddy had the opportunity of working toward these goals while she worked for the Human Rights Commission. These were exciting times seeing Chapter 15 section of the Constitution translated into laws. In the 90's Paddy was one of a team of human rights 'experts' invited to Ottawa to meet with representatives of the Indonesian government. They were there to discuss the introduction of human rights to Indonesia. Paddy retired in 2000 and has spent her time since enjoying her retirement by writing memoir and travelling. To date she has visited 15 countries from Europe to Africa. Not for her the nightlife, she prefers talking in the market places to local folk about their lives. Being a storyteller she can then spread the word about the plight of other when she gets home. She will continue to do this until she becomes too decrepit to travel!

NANCY STRIDER

Nancy Strider brings a different coming out story to Quirk-e. In the early nineties, her soul-mate husband found the courage to leave his very deep closet and start to live openly as a gay man. The next decade was spent lovingly deconstructing their marriage, in an effort to mitigate the losses. They remain active parents together. Nancy returned to prioritizing her creative work as a visual artist. Now, thanks to Quirk-e, she is taking her writing seriously, too. Interested in the shifts that come with aging, she examines turning points, hones her way-finding skills, takes notes, and makes maps.

HARRIS TAYLOR

Harris Taylor is a documentary filmmaker who moved to Whitehorse, Yukon after reading "the Northern Lights have seen queer sights." Having observed this environmental truth, she made television, love and trouble across the Canadian north and now, makes art with Quirk-e.

Photo by Helen Fallding

CHRISTINE WAYMARK

Trains that are bombed, planes with engines
    on fire and bunking in steerage on an
    ocean liner,
I dream still of travelling far.
TechnoGran to my family, including 2
    great-grandchildren,
I embrace the many ways to stay in touch.
Ritual, Rights, Relationships,
Threads that will never end.
The tapestry of my life is a rainbow of colour,
    and rich in texture.